HAPPILY EVER AFTER

HSING YUN'S HUNDRED SAYINGS SERIES

HAPPILY EVER AFTER
VENERABLE MASTER HSING YUN

HSI LAI UNIVERSITY PRESS
HACIENDA HEIGHTS, CALIFORNIA

ISBN 0-9642612-1-9
Library of Congress Catalog Card 95-76173

Printed in the United States of America

CONTENTS

Preface

The sutra states:

> Merit from donating the seven treasures
> of the great chiliocosm of three kinds of
> thousands of chiliocosms will not equal
> that attained in upholding a four-line
> verse of wisdom.

What exactly does it mean? There will be the day, the Buddha is telling us, when the riches we donate are exhausted, but the donation of knowledge, skill, truth, and the Dharma treasure is limitless in use and withdrawal.

Sometimes a few words, like a four-line verse, would suffice to impact on an entire life.

I had seen *Universal Gate* magazine seeking readers' submission of one-line verses of wisdom. I had also seen newspapers and periodicals featuring quotable quotes by illustrious characters. Without a doubt, whether it be a mere single-line verse or a few brief words, countless lives could still be touched. Many a time I would feel the urge to share those few words with the greatest influence on me. However, after giving it a little more thought, I realized that, rather than conveying in my own words recollections of the past, I would really want to collect the many words of encouragement given me by those benevolent teachers and gracious acquaintances in my life. The book which resulted would be one way of showing my appreciation to those individuals. Such is the motivation behind *Hsing Yun's Hundred Sayings Series*.

Looking back into the past brings manifold emotions. I remember how, upon hearing Venerable Chih Fêng utter the line: "Don't become the withered bud or rotten seed of Buddhism!" I not only committed myself to the Bodhisattva mind, but also made my Bodhisattva vow; and how, upon hearing Venerable Master Chih K'ai say: "Spread the Dharma to benefit all living beings!" I never let myself forget the formidable responsibility toward humankind that I must shoulder or the mission that my master assigned me.

In my youth, I was once called an underachiever. That drove me to vow to live up to my potentials. Worse, I was deemed useless. But it spurred me on. There was never any doubt in my mind that I can always make up personal weaknesses by added diligence and become a person of worth!

In the days gone by, many encouraged and praised me, or slandered and criticized me. Be they out of kindness or otherwise, their words invariably all became positive causes and conditions along my path toward cultivation. They also formed the favorable and unfavorable – but always facilitating – conditions enabling me to learn how to conduct myself in life.

As paddies produce crops of rice, and in mud thrives the immaculate lotus, the state of the objective environment is not nearly as important as our being a healthy seed. For only a good seed produces good fruit. One must allow the springs, summers, autumns, and winters, the winds, frosts, rains, and snows to become causes and conditions of one's growth. Through all objective vicissitudes, we must never lose sight of growth and progress as our purpose in life. Today, I rejoice at being in possession of personal worthiness and virtue, affinity with many people, as well as correct perception and knowledge. For this I thank the Buddha's benevolence and the kindly conditions from all ten directions.

In *Hsing Yun's Hundred Sayings Series*, I do not want to indulge in lofty eloquence or see any words and phrases wasted. I only want to contain snippets from my past and my thoughts in the one-line verse from which I have benefited greatly as a verification of the meaning of life. Sometimes I do not feel as if I entirely understand the circumstances in which I find myself. At other times, because of my advanced years and failing memory, remembrances of bygones are beginning to fade. It is those fervent devotees who, by asking to hear about my past, keep prodding me on. I am willing to leave them with some personal reminiscences. That is, while I am still able to speak and write of them. May those disciples who followed me into monasticism find among *Hundred Sayings* some guidelines in life and inspirations for their future.

Starting in July 1992, I began contributing monthly to the *Hundred Sayings* column in *Universal Gate* magazine. The entire collection of *Hundred Sayings* will probably take ten years in all. Completion of such an undertaking – a marathon in life – will have to depend on how long I am able to run, how far I am able to walk!

To date, sixteen pieces out of the hundred were written. To comply with everyone's wishes, these shall go to press,[1] while the rest will wait for another day.

Lastly, I would like to thank *Global News Monthly* and *Universal Gate* magazines for featuring these articles from *Hundred Sayings*, and Reverend Man Kuo, a graduate in accounting from Fu Jen University and a graduate from Fo Kuang Shan Buddhist College, for her help in recording my words. But most of all, I would like to convey my sincerest gratitude to the Triple Gems of all directions and the devotees preserving the Dharma, without whose contributions *Hsing Yun's Hundred Sayings* would simply never be.

Hsing Yun
Founder's Quarter,
Fo Kuang Shan, Taiwan
August 18, 1993

[1] Two texts of a total of thirty articles have been published in the Chinese language. Volume 1 of the English translation, *Perfectly Willing*, is a shortened compilation of ten articles from the first Chinese text, the remaining six articles of which are collected in Volume 2, *Happily Ever After*, together with four from the second Chinese text.

Acknowledgments

Among the many who have helped keep *Happily Ever After* on track, mention is hereby made of the following for their respective roles in the publishing of the second volume in *Hsing Yun's Hundred Sayings Series*: developmental editor Reverend Man Ho, translator Amy Lui-Ma who also researched for and wrote the footnotes in this translation, copyeditor May Lui, and book designer and prepress coordinator Anthony Ma. Further, special thanks are due to Reverend Yi Kung, vice-president of Hsi Lai University and abbess of Hsi Lai Temple, without whose support this translated text would not have been possible.

THE ESSENCE OF
PRACTICE

Venerable Master Yin Shun's[1] jolting remark on practice had stayed with me through forty years. What he said to me the day he arrived in Taipei from Hong Kong would always come back as a faithful admonition: "These days it looks as if everybody is claiming committal to the cause of practice, while in fact *practice* is just another word for indolence!" Such superbly insightful words could only have come from a genuine master, and they never ceased to prompt me in my efforts as a diligent practitioner.

I remember another time when Venerable Master Tao Yüan spoke on *The Awakening of Faith*[2] at Fo Kuang Shan. As I walked him back to his quarter at the end of the event, quite unexpectedly he gave a hearty outcry: "Practice! Practice! It looks like over-practice is fast eating away the Buddhist faith!" Such foresight could only have been envisaged and expressed by a compassionate

---

[1] All Chinese names in this text are romanized by the Wade-Giles system except for a few that are established in Pin-yin.

[2] A foundation work of Mahayana Buddhism.

Bodhisattva so deeply concerned as he with the maladies of the times.

Where be Buddhism

Through the years I came to visit many progressive countries where I saw church buildings lining boulevards and religious artifacts displayed with pomp in museums. I heard the nationals of a Christian country invariably stressing the faith of their land and those of an Islamic country living daily in praise of Allah. Back home, however, religion is more of a dispensable item. Some of our Buddhist leaders seem the least concerned with disseminating the Dharma and benefiting others, with life and happiness in this world, or with sacrifice and contribution. Instead they are committed to self-cultivation and self-preservation, and to practicing in the mountains or in seclusion. This explains the decline of Buddhism – why it is unable to prevail, practice is separated from daily living, and the Truth is removed from the masses at large, while the perverted is rampant, and superstition and ignorance are rife. Who should be held responsible for all of these?

Buddhism in China had been going downhill since the Ming and Ch'ing dynasties. Political prosecution had driven the religion from the community back into the mountains, and from public preaching and outreach programs back toward the direction of hermetic practice and self-cultivation. Fortunately for today though, with the dedicated vigor of Buddhist leaders and protective support of devotees, Buddhism is seen to enter an epoch of renewed growth.

Some of us, however, are not very perceptive of what is happening before them. They insist on practice in solitude over their responsibilities as a Buddhist, ignore the spiritual well-being of the devotees only to attend to their own, and neglect their social obligations, throwing away such essential building blocks of accomplishments as good causes, good affinities, and good deeds. Should everybody depart to practice in the mountains, who would deliver the sentient beings from their sufferings? And, what would become of the Buddhist faith?

Once a devotee asked me: "Master, if all of you should practice in solitude, who would there be to teach us and guide us toward liberation?"

Practice is No Excuse for Idleness

Practice is so important! But then, practice must not be used as a means of escape from reality or a tool of self-glorification. Practice is not some hollow slogan but a genuine, feet-on-the-ground dedication to self-perfection and self-sacrifice.

More than fifty years since I left the household life, regrets I still have a few over the triflingness of livelihood: my wisdom and insight remain inadequate, and my practice has not been rigorous enough. But never have I used practice as an excuse for idleness. Instead, I have devoted myself to the service of others, to responsibilities, and to hard work.

While in training at various monasteries, whether it be the vinaya school at Ch'i-hsia Shan (Cloud-dwelling Mountain),[3] the precept hall at Pao-hua Shan (Precious Flowers Mountain), the Buddhist college at Chiao Shan (Scorched Mountain), or the meditation hall in T'ien-ning (Heavenly Peace) Temple at Chin Shan (Golden Mountain), and whether

[3] In this text Chinese proper names, especially names of places and institutions, are given first in transliteration and then in bracketed translation unless stated otherwise.

it be the training in discipline or doctrine, I had striven for perfection. Whether it be joining others in chanting services in the hall, in outdoor labor, in serving in the kitchen or dining hall, in participating in summer and winter retreats, in attending the shrine, or in chopping firewood and fetching water, I had devoted myself wholeheartedly. Swiftly went ten years as I served the hundreds in the temples, day after day, and year after year. I know not if I could quite call it practice. Nonetheless those formative years were spent with much Dharma joy.

Really, the physical strenuousness of those days was next to nothing compared to the incredibly impoverished conditions. Livelihood in China then was meager beyond words as the country struggled desperately to get back on its feet from years of war and turmoil. It was one vast land of destitution. Often provisions were simply too scant to feed all the monks. Watery gruel, thin soup, soy bean dregs mixed with sand and bird droppings, and bug-infested dried turnip would have to make do. Thus we went for years without a decent meal, not to mention enough to keep warm or full. We mended our clothing with paper and glue; worn shoes

were repaired with chips of wood; and rags
others threw away were retrieved and worn
as socks for tatters were better than none. For
a long, long time I went without a cent on me.
I remember writing letters to my mother and
holding onto them in a batch. Come the
following year, I would write some more and
then hold onto them for yet another year.
This seemed to go on without end because I
never could afford the postage.

Trees in the Forest Thrive
on Their Own

Material poverty was, again, nothing
compared with the psychological pressure
of those apprenticing years. Trenchant
reproaches, rude demands, ruthless morti-
fication, and forced silence I took for the
integral parts of training. With neither grudge
nor remorse I accepted them as the *integral*
groundwork of monastic practice.

Young as I was in those days, I enthused
in the intensification of practice and the
verification of the Buddha's teachings. But at
the realization that I had no real contributions
to humanity or the temple, I refrained from

any selfish notions of leaving to practice on my own. So I adopted a form of practice that would not interfere with daily responsibilities: I ate one meal before noon each day, copied the sutras using my blood as ink, carried out the prostration drill late at night, practiced meditation, remained in silence for periods as long as one year, closed my eyes so as not to see, retreated on holidays, and locked myself up to concentrate on the Buddhist teachings. These exercises did not bring me enlightenment, but they bolstered my aspiration for and faith in Buddhism.

This I must tell the young students of today: I, in the course of learning and practice, had never sought to leave the monastic community for the indulgence of lone seclusion. For practice is what one does quietly and diligently in one's daily life; it is no cause to be boastful. A fledgling who takes its flight out of the nest before maturation would be incapable of finding its way home. For aspiring practitioners, the monastic community would remain their most wonderful training ground for as long as the training should take.

I arrived in Taiwan in 1949, without a

cent to my name, to confront the near impossibility of finding a shelter. Finally, a temple in Chungli took me in. Out of gratitude I began serving the others by undertaking the most menial tasks of pulling the cart, buying groceries, fetching water, cleaning the latrines, and tending the woods. Once better settled, I began to write and to travel widely teaching and spreading the Dharma.

Fo Kuang Shan was founded in 1967 in the hope of disseminating the Buddhist teachings to society at large. We lived during the beginning among thorny bushes and bamboos, and through rains and floods. Slowly, despite unrelenting financial constraints, social, educational, and cultural programs took form. Avowed to develop my Bodhi mind, obstacles of all kinds I would take for the integral lessons of practice.

In 1985 I left for a half-year seclusion in the United States after my retirement to allow for a smooth administrative transition. Since then, apart from teaching disciples, I have been employed fully, bustling around the globe, preaching the Dharma, building new temples, and accommodating the monastic

community. In 1992, in the hope of per-
meating the universe with the Dharma, I
established Buddha's Light International
Association.

Not Letting Go of the Sentient Beings

When I look back through the vista of the
past, life seemed to have elapsed in all those
attempts of mine to make the most out of
every moment. Although I regret not having
studied the Buddhist Canon as thoroughly as
I might or generated wisdom as deep as the
ocean, I know I have incorporated my
understanding of the Buddhist teachings in
daily life – not accumulating wealth but
giving freely, and not demanding unrea-
sonably of others but taking on the
responsibilities myself. Content with
simplicity, plain rice and tea feed me well no
matter how hectic the day is. At ease under
any circumstance, I can rest on any floor,
study in any cubicle, or compose on the road.
I help keep others on track, fulfill their
wishes, endure hardships, brush aside
criticisms, never tire of teaching or bringing
others happiness, am thankful for favors and

blessings bestowed upon me, am forgetful and forgiving of past animosities, keep time and promises, uphold ideals, am fearless of adversities, and, with one mind and one focus, practice according to the principles of Buddhism.

Much as I pay respect to the Buddha and follow him, however, I have no wish of becoming a Buddha; I practice giving without any wish of ascending to the heavens; and I uphold the Buddha's name but do not aspire for rebirth in the Lotus Land.[4] My resolution is to accumulate more resources for the path of the Buddha, not to transcend life and death; and my wish is to be reborn again and again in the saha world[5] as a monk with a nondiscriminatory mind.

Just how can life and death ever be easily concluded and relinquished? No one has ever made it without undertaking the cycles of life and death through innumerable kalpas.[6] Venerable Master T'ai Hsü equated

---

[4] The Pureland of Amitabha Buddha in the West to which rebirth is sought through the lotus-womb.

[5] The secular world.

[6] Age; aeon. A fabulous period of time in the Buddhist concept between the creation and recreation of a world or universe.

perfecting one's humanity with the attainment of Buddhahood in these simple words: "The perfecting of a person is the perfection of Buddhahood." The sixth patriarch of Ch'an[7] had taught that "the realization of the Dharma is here in the human realm." My attempt is to follow their teachings, put them into practice, and promote humanistic Buddhism. We do not have to abandon society in search for the way of the Buddha. To propagate the Buddha's teachings in society *is* a means of practice. Similarly, to serve society at large, to observe the Five Precepts[8] and the Ten Virtuous Deeds,[9] to uphold Right View and Right Faith, to give to the needy, to be compassionate and generous, and to uphold the Four Universal Bodhisattva Vows[10] *are* the ways of practice. The Buddha in his time had

[7] Venerable Master Hui Neng of T'ang dynasty.

[8] The five fundamental prohibitions: against killing, stealing, adultery, lying, and intoxicants.

[9] The ten good characteristics defined as the noncommittal of the ten evils: killing, stealing, adultery, lying, double-tongue, coarse language, filthy language, covetousness, anger, and perverted view.

[10] To deliver all living beings however limitless; to end all defilements however innumerable; to learn all methods however endless; and to become perfect in the supreme way of the Buddha.

not forsaken one sentient being; in the same token, humanistic Buddhism should not depart from any one way of the world. Walking, dwelling, sitting, and resting, arching the brow and blinking the eye, a thought rising and a remembrance returning, expounding and teaching, benefiting and delighting – which of these can be discounted as practice? Why do we, as Buddhists, have to turn our back on society? Why do we profess to live above and beyond this world and call it *practice*?

Practice! Practice! Appropriately we shall practice: by way of genuine acts of cultivation, virtue, compassion, good karma, and wisdom, so that all living beings in the dharma realms shall be enabled to practice properly; our minds, lives, and beings be filled with the Dharma; and this world be permeated with the Dharma.

RECORDS OF REPENTANCE

皆

大

歡

喜

Guilt and shame take over me each time I chant those lines of repentance:

> Sins committed in the past are,
> Without beginning, from greed, anger,
>   and ignorance,
> And born of behavior, discourse, and
>   thought.
> Today, for all of these, I must repent.

I am sixty-seven years old[1] and, looking back, I do see many causes for repentance.

Reflections on Sources from Which I Did Drink

I was ten when China went to war with Japan. That year my father left home on business, and the family had no word of him since. I never got to look after him in his old age; nor did I ever hold a memorial ceremony in his honor. This son shall forever be remiss in his filial duties! At age twenty-three I moved to Taiwan and had lost contact with my mother for the next four decades. Taking care of her material needs today does not

[1] In 1994.

alleviate the guilt of a son who had failed to attend her daily through many years. Efforts to channel the same heartfulness into relieving needy folks from home and to sublimate personal piety into the broad service of all living beings cannot begin to solace myself. Those efforts can never make up for my incompetence in filial duties.

I was my grandmother's pet. The first few years after I left home for the temple, I missed her so much that I would cry until dawn and tears would soak my pillow. News of her death came when I was barely settled in Taiwan. The remembrance of the instructions she had personally given me for her funeral, which I failed completely to fulfill, renders me heart-stricken. The remembrance of her being responsible for the causes and conditions that inducted me into the study of Buddhism is such a wrench. Now that I have obtained deliverance in the Dharma wherever has she transmigrated?

Master Chih K'ai was the mentor who bestowed upon me the body of spirituality and life of wisdom. He and I parted in 1949, and I had never heard from him again. On returning to visit some years back, I learned that Master Chih K'ai was brutalized in the Cultural Revolution and had perished. There was little else left for me to do except the care of his bereaved family. I have no words for the torment he must have been subjected to during his final days when I was nowhere around to attend to his needs or even ask after him as a pupil should, and for his gracious guidance and everything that he will always mean to me.

I was compelled to leave behind my two disabled chickens and skinny little native dog when I left home. I wonder where they had ended up and if they found peace for themselves. Amidst the bygones banished to dust, traces of remorse still linger. I also remember well, as I was set to leave the then war-torn country, how I kept only what was on my back and distributed the rest of my belongings to friends and relatives. For some time the thought of having acted as an open-handed giver of favors kept me walking on air. When I think of it now, I realize that the things given away then were in fact of no use to me anyway. How deplorable was such ugliness of the mind!

I remember having benefited most

exceptionally from the conscientious tuition of Venerable Shêng P'u at the Buddhist college in Chiao Shan. For two semesters he was the instructor of the Chinese language there. In 1989 when I went home I was so anxious to see him once again and to thank him in person. But, as things turned out, there was regretfully little way I could find time for the visit and I was merely able to entrust others to deliver gifts and greetings.

In 1948 a group of young monks – all believers and advocates of humanistic Buddhism – came to Hua-ts'ang Temple, Nanjing. I certainly was among them. Back then the group was feared like roaring floods and ferocious beasts by the traditionalists. Yet with benevolence the abbot Venerable Yin Yün received us and, before long, turned over to us the charge of the entire temple. These past years I have tried in vain to get in touch with him – a compunction unto this day.

In my youth I had studied at Buddhist colleges in Ch'i-hsia, Chiao Shan, and other places, under the tuition of some eminent masters the memory of whom I will always cherish: Venerable Jung Chai's support and guidance; Venerable Chih Fêng's maxim:

"Don't become the withered bud or rotten seed of Buddhism;" Venerable Shêng P'u's influence and encouragement; and the wealth of worldly knowledge handed down to me by Chieh Ju and P'u Lien. What a pity it is that I have learned without true clarity of mind and that I have failed to apply judiciously all that I learn. Thus forever indebted to the graciousness of the masters, how can I help feeling just as remorseful?

For years I had also trained at Ch'an meditation halls in Chin Shan, Ch'angchou, and other places. I had meditated in seven-day Pureland retreats and attained to the experience of selflessness. The tireless induction of Masters Shuang T'ing and T'ai Ts'ang of Chin Shan, Chêng Lien of T'ien-ning Temple, and Chih Kuang of Chiao Shan had brought me the joys of the Dharma and meditation. But, I am still at a loss for total enlightenment. And my mind[2] is a long, long way from the state of clarity. That the kindness of the eminent masters is yet to be reciprocated puts me to such shame.

I had concentrated my faculties on chanting from dawn till dusk during winter

[2] From which all things, or thoughts of things, arise.

seven-day retreats at the Buddhist colleges in Ch'i-hsia Shan and Chiao Shan, during each and every weekend service through all the years in Taiwan, and during the hundred or more seven-day Pureland retreats I was asked to conduct. After all that I suppose I can say that I do know a little about the method of chanting. But then again, how I must lament not having sufficiently applied myself or accomplished anything in accordance with the strength of the vows of Amitabha Buddha![3]

In self-discipline and self-improvement neither do I feel that, as a Buddhist monastic, I have lived up to all of 250 precepts.[4] Not even in the five major precepts, in fact, have I attained to the state of completeness and pureness!

A Scrutiny of the Past for Regrets

Fishing with childhood playmates had brought great thrills. But thoughts of the frantically jerking fish and shrimps still haunt

---

[3] Buddha of Infinite Light and Life. He receives to his Pureland in the West whoever calls on his name. This is the fulfillment of the eighteenth of his forty-eight vows.

[4] Rules for a fully ordained Buddhist monk.

me. Another time a viper did perish under my club. For a while I even delighted in my feat as the folks at home used to say: "The merit of destroying one viper surpasses that of abiding by the vegetarian discipline for ten years." But on leaving home to study Buddhism, I soon realized the existence of equality among all living beings and of interdependence among the causes and conditions for every phenomenon in the dharma realms. Remorse overtook me for what I had committed. In this world of ours, after all, it is so hard to pinpoint who in fact is hurtful to whom. The past two decades had seen me with a much revised attitude: I would, at best, drive a stray roach or fly that crossed my path out the door, and I would feed and release questing mosquitoes and ants that came into view. But none of these could ever have compensated for the grim wrongfulness of messing with the creatures in the water or slaying that viper!

I recall having once picked up a leather wallet and, as a child, becoming quite beside myself in glee. In another incident, we were touring the Tunhuang Caves,[5] Kansu

[5] A majestic treasure house of Buddhist relics and frescoes.

province, China, in 1989 with a group from International Buddhist Progress Society when a disciple found among the rubble a thin wooden chip, which we took for a remnant of antiquity. I, too, saw what was done and rejoiced in what seemed to be the fortune of the moment. But on reflection, I shudder at such inferior acts of wanton theft. And the realization of our incompetence in preserving treasured cultural relics adds to my contrition.

Never for once had I crossed the boundary of worldly love and affection, but compassion and regard for others I have always embraced. This, being the way of the Bodhisattva, must have accorded with the heart of the Buddha. But in the way of the Hinayana,[6] it is perhaps a bit of a fuss. As advanced in years as I, I cannot honestly comment on the favors, grudges, affections, and hostilities of this world, but shall seek to repent before all the Buddhas hereafter.

I have a lifelong detestation for smoking and drinking. But then, I never did quite speak up against the two vices as devotees

---

[6] Lesser Vehicle. The division or school of Buddhism seeking destruction of defilement and extinction in nirvana.

would time and again request me to because I did not regard myself sufficiently seasoned in the ways of the world to do so. Thinking back, I simply cannot hope to evade the blame of not living up to my responsibility in societal purification.

Just how can I profess to be a teacher and role model to the humans and devas, when I am myself as wanting as this in the observance of the Five Precepts? I am ashamed to be a Tathagata[7] disciple, and I am ashamed to be robed in the attire of a monastic!

For a decade I had conducted the *Mêng-shan* services,[8] and for many years, innumerable ceremonies for the dead and penitential services. The diligently flowing recitation of the *Great Compassion Mantra*[9] and the ten short mantras therein had seen them converge in the ocean of my mind. But then, I was capable of no more than the ready employment of the esoteric incantations in everyday life – a

---

[7] Absolute Come. *Ju-lai* in Chinese. One of the titles of a Buddha.

[8] Evening services for the deliverance of those from the hells.

[9] An incantation against defilement.

supplementary practice which, though conducted in spontaneity, was not intended to resonate with the three esoterics of the Buddha,[10] and hence was yet to bring about enlightenment of any form. How I had squandered all that time!

Through fifty years of monastic life I have never ceased to quest for self-improvement – from daily exercises and ascetic practice to community service; from seclusive study to wide travels; from chanting and meditation to preaching the Dharma; and from charity to educating the masses. I used to take pride in decades of endeavors in the ways of humanistic Buddhism – writing, publishing, educating the young, supporting the needy, relieving the poor and disabled, and introducing the Dharma into homes, neighborhoods, communities, and states. I thought that, in irrigating the five continents with the flow of the Dharma and thus nourishing all living beings in the dharma realms, I would in earnest be upholding the Four Noble Truths[11] and Eightfold Noble

---

[10] Namely, the Buddha's action, discourse, and thought.

[11] The fundamental doctrines of Sakyamuni Buddha: suffering, its cause, its cessation, and the Eightfold Noble Path (see the following note).

Path[12] of the Buddha. But upon close examination of the past, I see vows that were not quite deep enough, sympathy not ardent enough, benevolence not encompassing enough, and resolve not vast enough. My efforts were a long, long way yet from the six paramitas[13] and the myriad modes of deliverance, not to mention the Four Universal Bodhisattva Vows of the Mahayana![14]

I have the utmost appreciation and admiration for Venerable Master T'ai Hsü's unwavering protection of the Dharma and sangha,[15] Master T'ai Ts'ang's affable countenance and good cheer, Master Miao Kuo's graciousness and magnanimity, Venerable Master Lcan-skyagegen's integrity and outspokenness, Master Tz'ŭ Hang's forthrightness and benevolence, and Master

[12] The eight right ways for a practitioner to nirvana (liberation from existence): right view, right thought, right speech, right action, right livelihood, right effort, right mindfulness, and right concentration.

[13] The six vehicles to liberation: charity, observance of the precepts, tolerance, zeal and progress, meditation, and wisdom (the power to discern reality).

[14] Larger Vehicle. The division or school of Buddhism aiming at universal Buddhahood, which means the perfect enlightenment of all sentient beings.

[15] The Buddhist monastic community.

Yin Shun's illustrious scholarly pursuits. While in quietude I pray for them, I fear that I am too wanting in good karma and virtue, causes and conditions to ever follow in their footsteps.

All my life I had never been disrespectful toward the masters and venerables. But some instances I just cannot seem to let go. Once I pounded on the desk before Master Nan T'ing out of a heated protest against the management of the Maitreya scholarships and the establishment of the Chih-kuang school of commerce. Another time I stormed out of an exasperating session with Master Tung Ch'u over disagreements on the article selection for *Jên-shêng yüeh-k'an* (Life Monthly).[16] Gracious as they were then, I can never quite forgive myself for what happened. However, my conscience will always be clear for having spoken up against Venerable Pai Shêng's dictatorial running of monastic affairs!

Turning to look myself in the eye, have I not often spoken against views not mine and in favor those of my own? As much as I speak

---

[16] All Chinese journal titles in this text are given first in italicized transliteration and then in bracketed translation.

out of justice for the Buddhist faith, or to lay the groundwork for or facilitate the preaching of the Dharma, I have to plead guilty for the excessiveness of my ways. While I strive hard to restrain myself, I likewise caution my disciples against committing the same blunder. But then, I am afraid I still have some self-disciplining to do!

Repentance is the Introspection of a Lifetime

Reception of the teachings of the masters since childhood had long affirmed my identity as a disciple of the Mahayana. Patterning my efforts upon the Bodhisattva spirit, I understand profoundly that the strength of a vow stems not from the improvisation of a moment but from the commitment of a lifetime, and that it is not to be contained within but fulfilled without. Never have I complained to the heavens or before fellow humans about stumbling blocks and hurdles along the path of making vows, establishing affinities, acting in compassion, and cultivating good karma and wisdom. But comes each night when I look within myself,

I deplore a mind that is yet to be cleared of its impurities[17] and for the continued presence of old habits. I keep reminding myself that repentance is not an occasional confession but the introspection of a lifetime, and not an ornamental declaration but the assiduous cleansing of greed, anger, and ignorance. But with the three roots[18] long sprung and the past karma already in place, how can I not repent in prostration and plead for the Buddha's forgiveness? Having written thus in self-scrutiny, I shall also intend this for the inspiration of those who follow.

[17] Defiling thoughts.

[18] Also called the three poisons: greed, anger, and ignorance. They are the source of all defiling thoughts, or passions and delusions.

ACROSS
TEN DIRECTIONS,
THROUGHOUT
THREE JUNCTURES

皆

大

歡

喜

People often ask me: "Just how does Fo Kuang Shan manage its enormous sangha and mammoth undertakings to achieve such oneness of heart and total harmony?"

At that I would cite a Buddhist expression, which goes: "Across the ten directions,[1] throughout the three junctures."[2]

Another time, pondered a journalist: "Would the charisma factor suffice to explain your popularity?"

I know little about personal charm. I am merely coping by way of the belief of "across the ten directions, throughout the three junctures." As well, this is one personal example I seek to pass onto disciples.

During those formative years in the monasteries, we were required to learn the Buddhist terminology by rote – without grasping much of the meaning. Little did I expect those seeds of wisdom, long sown in

---

[1] Of space, i.e., the eight points of the compass together with the nadir and zenith, the lowest and highest points.

[2] Past, present, and future.

the field of the eighth consciousness,[3] would in time come to flourish at the spur of sundry causes and conditions. How wondrous is the application of the Dharma! How ineffable! The axiomatic "across the ten directions, throughout the three junctures" I find to be especially descriptive of the Dharma body and wisdom-life,[4] and infinitely viable in the running of everyday affairs.

By the *Dharma body and self-nature* it means the essential Buddhahood within us. Across the span of space, everything on earth has its implicit limitation except the Truth, the Dharma body, and wisdom as life, which are vast without the outermost, minute without the innermost, and ever-present. Hence "across the ten directions." Throughout the course of time, as the physical body undergoes life and death in various forms of rebirth, the true mind and self-nature shall override the limit of past, present, and future – undying, nonexistent, and absolute. Hence

---

[3] The eight consciousness are: seeing, hearing, smelling, tasting, touch, intellect, discrimination, and the store house, which is the source of all seeds of consciousness or perception.

[4] Body of spirituality and wisdom as life; the essence of being.

"throughout the three junctures." In a nutshell, in the Dharma body and self-nature lies the never-changing and forever-new Truth, and across the ten directions and throughout the three junctures, its universal application.

My own comprehension of "across the ten directions, throughout the three junctures" is such that, for everything to be said or done, think twice. Be sure to cover each and every interrelationship between this matter and that, between this person and that, and among reflections and projections of the past, present, and future.

At times someone would come to me with a grumble, saying, "The others think my work isn't up to par."

"What's their point?" I would ask.

"I'm told I should have talked things over with others beforehand."

"So, what you've done falls short of 'across the ten directions!'"

Or, another would confess, saying, "I'm told that the way I handle the Dharma function isn't in accordance with propriety."

"But why is that so?"

"I'm blamed for having acted ruthlessly, without ever consulting superiors or referring to past records, and blundered badly as a result."

"So, you aren't exactly following the way that's 'throughout the three junctures.' That's why!"

Across the ten directions, throughout the three junctures; all shall be well. And vice versa.

After my retirement from Fo Kuang Shan, Abbot Hsin Ping who succeeded me would still consult me on some of the major functions, saying, "How should we go about doing it this year?"

"Just refer to past records," I would say.

Such a reply may sound routine, but there is really more to it. For things done in those early years were in fact manifestations of my personal ideals. While attention is paid to tradition, which in turn should resonate with the religious spirit, emphasis is equally placed on progress and innovation alongside changing times. We must *refer to* – instead of abide by – the past, in itself an exemplification that is "throughout the three junctures." Changes of all forms always call for deliberation, agreement, and eventual communication. In the process, meetings are an indispensable mechanism. There had not been anything, since the inception of Fo Kuang Shan, which was not resolved in a meeting and in a democratic manner. As a result of meetings "across the ten directions" – among employees, executives, departments, and even students – affairs at Fo Kuang Shan are run so much more smoothly, and those who participate are able to come away with forever bettering communication skills.

On occasion I would have reports of incompetence: "I'm reprimanded for having been remiss in the reception of visitors."

"What seems to be the problem?"

"I've been tardy in sundry chores: opening the door, turning on the lights, preparing tea, and notifying the departments concerned."

"So, you aren't exactly following the way that's 'across the ten directions, throughout the three junctures.' That's why!"

An acute perceptiveness was the fruition of years of management experience in the monastic workplace, particularly in the area of public relations. I learned, at the rise of a circumstance, to associate one point with the others, to line up all the factors, and to contemplate the circumstance in its entirety which, aptly timed and spaced, will never go awry. Thus I ensured that my disciples in those early years were rightly trained. Many of them are today top-notch communicators and coordinators.

In communicating via time and space as much as humanistic bonding, the perceptive "across the ten directions, throughout the three junctures" equally applies. Disciplinarian aside, I must say I am a *people-person*, too, with disciples. Take, for instance, the dilemma of having two performers who are equally commendable, with only one award to give. A solution would be requesting one to deliver the award to the other: "I would appreciate it if you could do me the favor of sending this gift on. You must also know that I shall be sure to make it up to you when another gift comes to hand." In such a case, one would be thrilled with the award and the other, with a healthy sense of self-worth. All would be well indeed.

Affinity Through Time

I can even say that it was on the perception of "across the ten directions, throughout the three junctures" that my character was built. Back in those school days, a good read, a few words of truth, or news of interest of any kind would invariably set me flitting among schoolmates with my amazing find, which I wanted to be sure everyone was there to share with me. I befriended many, many that way. Even now, a flashing idea or some opportune thought I will not hesitate to share with friends and followers, and hope what crosses my mind may equally inspire others. And, sights and sounds from every journey I always bag and bring home.

I have always believed that communication is the miracle drug of good affinity and bonding is the facilitating condition[5] that promotes growth. But to my

---

[5] A Buddhist term. The condition by which advancement to a higher stage is made.

plea for intercollegiate exchanges among the Buddhist institutions as far back as a decade ago, a generally deaf ear was turned. What a pity that everybody seemed so jealous of one's own interests!

In the Sino-Thai Buddhist conference of 1964, I had proposed that solidarity, unification, and mobilization be our focus, and a consensus was reached. Through the years, I continue to urge cooperation among the Buddhist communities, hoping that citadels be founded upon unanimity and energy be sublimed in concentration. For devotees there are chanting sessions, youth groups, women's groups, Ch'an meditations, and Vajra groups for male volunteers; for the academia, annual international Buddhist scholarly exchanges; and among the Buddhist schools, inter-disciplinary gatherings such as the World Sutric and Tantric Conference of 1985 and the Ch'an, Pureland, and Tantric joint function of 1993. Successes all of them have been. And immensely acclaimed, too. For an act that accords with the method of the Truth is never in vain.

The concept of space implicit in "across the ten directions" broadens the mind, and that of time in "throughout the three junctures" expands the vision. In the same token, I have every respect for convention while I will not hesitate to flow with the times. I had been critical of unauthorized changes pertaining to the celebration of the Buddha's birthday, but had also championed the revision of the monastic liturgy. I remain verbal against linking the Buddhist faith with secular worship of the deities, and continue to call for the clear delineation of quasi-Buddhists. Over the elaboration of the methods of cultivation I advocate a simplified liturgy that is in no way amiss in solemnity for the benefit of the masses. Without fail, through twenty-eight years of running the Buddhist college, we have adhered to each and every daily routine in the most traditional format: the morning bell and evening drum, the early and late liturgy, the gathering of firewood and fetching of water, and the receiving of guests and serving at meals. Meanwhile, teaching patterns are consistently to keep in step with the times, and students always to be prodded toward independent thinking.

For a long time my disciples and I had biked deep into the country to propagate the Right Belief in the Dharma. These days, of course, we bustle about in the *hi-tech* convenience of autos and jets. Even so, the apropos revival of some good old ways still comes across as the germane illustration of the Dharma. Launched in 1989, the age-old alms procession is held at Fo Kuang Shan every other year to allow devotees the opportunity to make offerings and sow seeds of good karma, and to bring upon the monastics themselves a simply wonderful experience. Here I must mention a traveling gala which we had staged in Taiwan since the Eighties. Called *Return to the Epoch of the Buddha*, the monumental congregation of all sentient beings at Gṛdhrakūṭa (Vulture Peak) 2,500 years ago to listen to the Buddha was reenacted with bedazzling special effects, showing tens of thousands of devotees the way back in time to bask once again in the Dharma joy of praising the Buddha. I only pray that forty years of preaching the Dharma, a continuation of the spirit of Tathagata throughout the three junctures, will be my legacy for posterity.

One for All and All for One

In religion, I am for all eight schools of thought; in politics, I am nonpartisan. I would like to think that, by the notion of "across the ten directions, throughout the three junctures," the universal gate (*p'u-mên*)[6] will always be flung open to all who come to benefit from the Dharma. I recall what a sensation it caused when I went home to be reunited with my mother, family, and friends in 1989. To everyone who came to greet me I offered a gift of affinity, praying that a moment's bonding would turn into a hope of salvation.

Many are somewhat bemused by this unflagging enthusiasm of mine in cultural ventures which appear, more often than not, to be a losing cause. But I have every faith in the prajna[7] of language, which forever passes on, and in education, which picks up from the past and opens new ways to the future. Not only do I continue to urge that the Buddhist classics be translated into the modern Chinese

---

[6] The unlimited doors open to a Buddha or Bodhisattva, and the forms in which a Buddha or Bodhisattva appears.

[7] Wisdom.

language, preachers of the Dharma be trained for the international podium, branch temples be built far and wide, practice and festivities to include all, and medicare to reach the indigent, but for myself, I never stop learning.

Insight into the Tripitaka[8] I may have little; the worldly erudition I may have none of. But on wings of the vastness of "across the ten directions, throughout the three junctures" I have never stopped perusing every book or journal that I chance upon, comparing and contrasting each good read with every experience, making cross-references between daily life and societal phenomena, and implementing all that I learn. In the process, I believe I am enabled to communicate to the masses what is correct, comprehensible, and discerning.

"Read through ten thousand scrolls; journey over ten thousand miles." On multiple occasions have I taken groups overseas for visits or on pilgrimages, and motivated disciples and students to travel and pay homage to the holy sites, so much so that,

---

[8] The Three Baskets. The entire Buddhist Canon consisting of the sutras, vinaya, and sastras.

throughout the three junctures in civilization, we are enabled to trace the veins of all cultural vicissitudes, and, across the ten directions of the world, to expand the terrain of experience.

In doing what must be done, I have abided by the permanent and followed the impermanent in accordance with the nature and essence of the Dharma. Many times I had stood up in defense of monasterial properties and in advocacy of democracy in the halls of government. And I would always pause to enquire after anyone nearby as much as I would take time to confer with party dignitaries. Madam Sun-Chang Ching-yang, a dear friend, had in her lifetime showered me with hospitalities. I was appreciative but not flustered. And in the wake of her passing, I gave all to this giant of a protector of the Dharma. The truth of the matter is that, I felt, across the ten directions and throughout the three junctures in the dharma realms permeated with the nature of the Buddha, the Buddha and I share in the selfsame nobleness of nature. I need not bend before might or be perplexed by wealth and nobility. In the meantime, I am one with all living beings. Let me preach to them from the lion throne[9] and toil as their cattle and horses.[10] Let me be large and small, forward and backward, with and without, rejoicing and suffering, stretching and bending, and full and wanting. I may not be omnipotent, but I am *willing and able*. It is the potency of my own nature that enables me to walk the expanse of heaven and earth, across the ten directions, throughout the three junctures.

Within the truthful "across the ten directions, throughout the three junctures" I have benefited profoundly, and would hope all living beings have a share of the same Dharma joy. The founding of Buddha's Light International Association in 1992 has since brought together devotees from around the globe in one concerted endeavor to leave this existence – across the ten directions – with the right tracks, and to leave this universe – throughout the three junctures – with kindness and sympathy.

[9] Wherever the Buddha is seated.

[10] Be at the service of the masses.

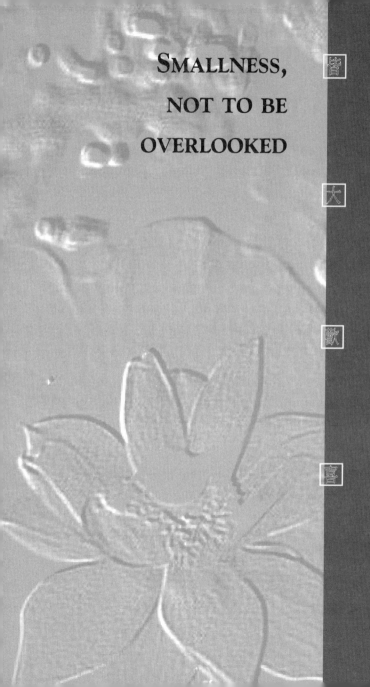

SMALLNESS,
NOT TO BE
OVERLOOKED

皆

大

歡

喜

We all tend to covet after the superlative: the bigger the better, or the more the merrier. Even in this age of high technology with its adoration for the incredible lightness – and slimness – of being, we look to the small and light for practicality only: books for the pocket, and minisedans for supermileage.

We tend to overlook the *little* people, things, and happenings which, as it turns out, bear in them an infinite sense of the future. Like sand and stones in concrete skyscrapers, or bolts and screws in mega production lines; a drop that erodes a rock, a spark that rages across a plain, or the sediment that stops up a flow; a comment on which the fate of a nation hangs, or a gift that relieves an emergency; a smile that reassures, a word that lends support, a daily good deed that brings wide affinities, or a story that inspires; a child who grows up to take the helm of society, or a young heir who succeeds a throne; an intolerance that thwarts a grand design. Nothing small, indeed, is to be ignored.

My mother had for years suffered from lingering ill health. At her bedside I used to read for her from the folkloric seven-word passages of old Yangchou and, as I did so, she would correct the words I mispronounced. The early lessons from my mother, who could not read herself, culminated into a lifelong ardor for reading. More important, from all that quality time with my mother sprang the strongest sense of loyalty, filiality, integrity, and justice. Through the course of time, childhood bonding with my mother took the form of causes and conditions for my aspiration to be a person of great virtue.

When I was a little older, I was sent off to a rural private school. One day I chanced upon a text belonging to one of the children attending the nearby English school. It read: "Off to school in shirt-sleeves and shorts, [let us] always [be] on the dot." I gobbled up the small wisdom, which laid the groundwork of my sense of punctuality and honor.

Afloat for fifty years in the ocean of the Dharma, I, too, have for many, many times come to savor from a mere gourdful its ineffable sweetness.

A Lot Begins with a Little

As a student in the monasteries, I would make

every salutation or prostration from the piety and reverence of the heart, and each consultation or report as propriety demanded. Memories of having waited for hours to be accommodated at Chin-shan Temple and for days to see the abbot of P'i-lu Temple will always be ineffaceable. From these lessons of acceptance, humility, and fortitude I had benefited immensely.

I had also been in the service of not a few masters, doing everything from waiting on meals thrice daily to standing by in the Dharma functions for the longest hours. The positions were physically very taxing indeed, but spiritually most rewarding. From the demeanor of the venerable masters I learned about pertinence, and from the odd jobs I realized the mighty working of the Dharma. Work, always onerous, never swamped me; and pressure, always mounting, did not get the better of me.

On the occasion of my tonsure, Master Jung Chai, whom I regarded with tremendous deference, gave me the Dharma name of Chin Chüeh (Instantaneous Awakening). He said to me: "Don't ever take the two characters lightly. Attainment of them will make you truly worthy of leaving home[1] to follow the path." I had since taken the two characters to heart and mused over them often. Later I would encourage students and followers to introspect daily: a little revelation each day will in time precipitate the great eventual enlightenment.

Being Master Chih K'ai's only disciple did not entitle me to any privileges but rather subjected me to much deepened austerity in training. A bout of malaria at age seventeen taught me one of the harshest lessons in aloneness and affliction. Then, just as I thought the end was near, someone came with a small bowl of salted vegetables from Master Chih K'ai for my thin gruel. Moved to the quick, I vowed to dedicate the rest of my life to the Buddhist faith. Now, how a bowl of salted vegetables would become the inspiration for a great vow might understandably sound far-fetched to some. Yet a little heartfelt gratitude did see me through tens of thousands of predicaments at which I never flinched. I would count that as one of the greatest gains in my life.

[1] Becoming a monk.

A Little Gratefulness Gathers into the Potency of Great Vows

At age eighteen I arrived at the gate of T'ien-ning Buddhist College in Ch'angchou to find enrolment quite full. So I ended up as an errand boy and waiting on meals. In the course of all this, a kindly preceptor gave me a pair of socks – the only gift I had ever received in those years of learning. Such a gift, small as it was, taught me one of the most indelible lessons in the merit of good affinities.

At age nineteen I came upon Chiao-shan Buddhist College to be greeted at the gate with smiles and amenities. The receptionist even took my luggage. A young monk then, I was utterly touched by such courtesy. The interlude impacted profoundly on me as a manifestation of what came to be a lifelong commitment of mine: *Make gifts of joy.*

At the outbreak of the civil war between the nationalists and communists in China in 1949, it was decided between a classmate and myself that he would stay with the temple and I would head for the then-outlandish Taiwan. We would proceed toward different directions but with the same dedication in the preservation of Buddhism. The pledge to give my utmost had seen me through the worst plights, and remembrances of the pact with my bosom friend had never failed to urge me on. After years of searching I finally caught up with him and, in honor of one unbreachable mutual commitment, have since furnished him with every support within my powers.

People envy me for the ability to face an ocean of an audience without a flutter. Frankly, it is the outcome of years of trials and errors in the countless small-scale sessions. I must mention the time in 1953 when I preached at Lei-yin Temple in Ilan at the invitation of Li Chüeh-ho. The green horn that I was then palpitated like a leaf before the audience and literally had to grab the edge of the table with both hands to steady myself! When at last it was over and I removed myself from stage, to my horror, I was soaked with sweat. As experiences added on, so did self-assurance and mien. Most of all, as much as I am moved by the fervor of the audiences today, I shall forever be indebted to those who had come to hear me in the days gone by for their benevolence and succor.

Once the Little Bodhisattvas, Now the Great Protectors of the Dharma

Taiwan, insulated as it was two to three decades back, had yet to tell the deities and the Buddhas apart. For the Right Belief of Buddhism to reach the masses, we had resorted to a range of innovative functions. One day, I was struck by the notion of the Buddha preaching with sounds so much so that I took to writing a collection of verses, which Yang Yung-p'u set to music. Eventually a choir was formed. As I preached, these animated youths virtually sang their way into the heart of a Taiwan which was still fairly rigorous in the Fifties, sowing seeds of the Bodhi[2] in their path. One simple tune after another became a powerful medium of communication. The lyrics touched a chord within many who did not even read much. Others, who were yet to be wonted to the complexity of the Dharma, became converted by the sheer zeal of the melodies. The songs and chanting were recorded. What a breakthrough in those days! And each small record became the vehicle that delivered the

[2] Perfect wisdom; the enlightened mind.

wondrousness of the Dharma to the doorstep of manifold homes.

Ilan Chanting Group was the bedrock of my collaboration with the devotees. Again and again the format was repeated elsewhere. Small-scale as they were, the groups had been receptive of all those who came to listen to the Dharma and to practice, and were instrumental in the making of many a Dharma body and wisdom-life. In the spring of 1992, I was in London, England, to launch a chapter of Buddha's Light International Association there. Vice-president Chao Li-chu, quite elated to see me, started to reminisce about something that had meant dearly to her – a gift of pen and papers from me ages back. Then we rambled onto what transpired through thirty-five years – from her father, president Chao Wang of Lung-yen Sugar Refinery, who formed chanting groups in his factory, to herself, whose dreams and aspirations now abound in propagating the Dharma on alien soil. How time had galloped on! Who would have guessed this gallant protector of the Dharma standing before me was the personable little girl I used to know! Moreover, those small-scale chanting groups of old were aggrandized into the supreme Dharma cause – one cause giving rise to another, and one generation handing down to the next!

In 1957 Chang Yu-li (later Reverend Tzu Hui) and Wu Suh-jen (later Reverend Tzu Jung) and the others pioneered the broadcast of the Dharma. The halfhour *Fo-chiao chih shêng* (The Buddhist Voice) they hosted on Min-pên (People's Own) Radio Station took off instantly, succeeded by another sensation, *Chüeh-shih chih shêng* (Sounds that Awaken the World) with China Broadcasting Corporation. Later on, one by one, all of these vernal team-players left home to become my disciples. From preaching at Lei-yin Temple in Ilan to founding Fo Kuang Shan in Kaohsiung, from setting up branch temples in every corner of Taiwan and around the globe to the launching of Buddha's Light International Association, and from the small chanting groups to the spectacular international functions – we have through thirty years gone from nonexistence to existence. Today, Hsin Ping has taken over the abbotship of Fo Kuang Shan, and Tzu Chuang, Tzu Hui, Tzu Jung, and Tzu Chia have all emerged from their youthful past to attain prominence in the Buddhist circle. Among them, Tzu Hui was the first-ever Bhiksuni[3] to assume vice-presidency in the World Fellowship of Buddhists.

It Always Begins from Page One

An avid reader since youthhood, I used to hide under my quilt at the start of the nightly grand silence to read and transcribe old texts with the light from an incense. I came to recite a good many literary masterworks and memorized innumerable celebrated verses. Light from the incense virtually enabled me to lay a fairly sturdy foundation in the classics.

While studying at Chiao-shan Buddhist College at age nineteen, one day, the surging Muse swept me off my feet. The result was the composition of a series of verse, which I submitted to *Chiangsu hsin-pao* (Chiangsu News Daily). This maiden publication – for

---

[3] Buddhist nun; Bhiksu, Buddhist monk. Defined as one who has left home and been fully ordained, and who depends on alms for a living. Hence almsman or almswoman.

one brief shining moment quite a stupe-faction to me – was the launching pad for my literary creativity.

At age twenty-three I did something else when I stood guard in the woods up the hills of Fa-yün Temple. It was on the frigid ground in the barren shed I penned *Wu shêng-hsi tê ko-ch'ang* (Singing in Silence). The book was a hit and, for my confidence, another impetus. Privately I pledged to carry on with my literary endeavors so that devotees would continue to bask in the verve of the Dharma.

At age twenty-five I was teaching Buddhism in Taiwan. Between classes, a colleague, Kuan K'ai-t'u, volunteered to give me and Venerable Yen P'ei private tuition in Japanese. It went on for six months. It was this humble beginning of mine in the Japanese language that had equipped me adequately to take on the formidable translation of the Japanese Buddhist text which Venerable Chih Tao later gave me. The joining of forces – among Wang Fa-lien who came up with the paper and Venerable Shêng Jui the funding, Venerable Shêng Yin who took over editing and Venerable Hsin Wu proofreading, and Venerable Chu Mo who rendered the calligraphy – hastened the publication of the flimsy volume of *Kuan-shih-yin P'u-sa P'u-mên-p'in chiang-hua* (Discourse on Avalokitesvara's[4] Universal Gate Chapter). This translated work in Chinese was the harmonizing of manifold causes and conditions which, once again, brought about the revelation of Avalokitesvara Bodhisattva at the Universal Gate indeed!

At age twenty-seven, in the cubicle in Lei-yin Temple and by the tiny light of the sewing-machine, I authored two major manuscripts: *Yu Lin kuo-shih* (National Master Yu Lin) and *Shih-chia-mou-ni Fo ch'uan* (Biography of Sakyamuni Buddha). The former was made into a motion picture and a miniseries for television. I honestly would not have expected this mere book be transformed into an electronic medium for the propagation of the Dharma. And, each word I wrote in the latter was to me a resonance with the Buddha and every line, a bonding. Further, the royalties I collected from the two texts expedited the purchase of properties and the construction of more temples. The

---

[4] Regarder of the World's Sounds. Protector of all in distress.

prajna of language in the form of a couple of books not only sustained wisdom as life, but also opened up a profusion of resources for the great cause of the Dharma.

In 1961 Chang Shao-chi and Chang Jo-hsü graciously entrusted me with *Awaken the World*. Thirty years into publishing this, the print-run has peaked at a hundred thousand today. Once every ten days the smallish journal continues to service readers and to hold the Buddha's light high around the globe.

The award-winning programs I produced on all three television networks in Taiwan since 1979 were, at the onset, made outside the studios. Soon, however, these became studio productions – with the networks picking up the tabs! Ultimately broadcasts were dubbed in foreign languages and moved overseas and the transcripts published. That is a prime exemplar of how an educational project, despite its humble beginning and limitations, will ultimately come out on top for its excellence of content. For the public needs it, and will not hesitate to show that need.

A good count of the Sunday classes in

Ilan all the way to the kindergartens and junior classes in the branch temples and the Chinese schools tells me that I have expended forty prolific years in child education. That "children are the masters of a nation's future" is certainly no cliche! The sprightly kids from the early classes have evolved into individuals agleam with achievements and procreative protectors of the Dharma. True that a kindergarten is but a preschool playground. But the kids, germanely groomed, will mature into individuals who are appreciative of the blessings in life and cognitive of the good of industriousness. What promise, then, awaits them and an entire nation!

Every little thing upon Fo Kuang Shan is close to my heart. Shrubs and plants that I grew have long prospered into luxuriant groves and shady woods. A dune that took shape on East Hill once prevented Hsin Ping and four young sramaneras[5] from a plunge into disaster. Bottles of pure water disseminated during the Mahakaruna[6]

---

[5] Novice monks.

[6] Great Compassion. A heart that seeks to deliver the suffering. Applied to all the Buddhas and Bodhisattvas, especially Avalokitesvara (Kuan-yin).

functions have provided resources of unceasing miracles. The mini wick relic on exhibition was to me a revelation of the Buddha during a pilgrimage to India and to the many who have beheld it, a source of faithful strength.

The Great Chiliocosm of Three Kinds of Thousands of Chiliocosms in a Speck

How could smallness be deemed unmentionable? Smallness is the emblem of the hope that is endless.

With fortitude, the meek among us shall ride the tide of time and surge ahead; with earnestness, the gigantic hand of history shall amass the minims of causes and conditions into towering feats; and with humility, any singular notion formed the compassionate Buddha shall bless. Through an eye is viewed the world in its entirety; through the nostrils is sniffed the scent of space; and in one microscopic cell is begotten the force of life.

Let us not ever dismiss a small good or permit a small evil. For every little step taken is a big stride along the path of worldly existence. And concealed in smallness is a potency not ever to be overlooked!

FEAR NOT IN THE FACE OF DEATH

The person I revere most will always be my maternal grandmother Madam Liu, who was violated in every sense of the word at the hands of the Japanese invaders. Her assailants attempted to sear her, hack her, and drown her. But, she survived.

"Fear not," she told me, "in the face of death."

Many a time in my own life had I verged on death but – I would forever be indebted to the wisdom of my grandmother – never was I afeared.

Every so often I am asked how I view life and death. On life, I would call mine fulfilled: to my faith I give all, and to the joy of the Dharma I commit each day. On death, I hold dear the many times I look it in the eye. On life and death, I have come to realize that, as much as life may not always be a cause to celebrate, death may not always be a cause to grieve.

I was an agile little boy – and intrepid, too. Once, coming upon a wide trench, I thought in my little mind that I could cross it in one flighty leap. I landed squarely in the trench, where a shattered bottle went straight through the web of my toes. Blood spurted, and, clumsily, I tore off a corner of my shirt to dress the wound. I did not see a doctor or anything, and in passing the wound healed on its own. Young as I was, grandmother's words were already ingrained in my mind, and impressions of her bravery kept me from the fear of death.

A Matter of One Breath

My hometown was nestled deep in the snow-belt. How my older brother and I used to have the time of our life frolicking in the snow and ice-skating on the river! One New Year's Eve, I – then barely eight – was taking a lone stroll on the icy river when, suddenly, I spotted what looked like a duck's egg lying aglint in the distance. I scurried forth to fetch the find – only to discover it to be a patch of thinning ice about to crack! Just as I swung around to flee, one of my feet had already trodden into the icy water. Then the whole of me just slipped in. Frenzied, I scrambled to get myself out but, within seconds, was chilled from head to toe. The very last thought I could recall was: "Boy, I'm through!" What transpired thereafter I had not the slightest inkling of. The next thing I knew, I was quivering – quite light in the head – in the bitter cold and knocking on our door. "Goodness, what happened to you?!" cried my brother, quite startled, as he answered it. I was practically frozen by then. But how I got out of the icy river I could not honestly remember. When pressed further, somehow, I seemed to recollect a personable old lady leading me to our doorstep.

I just turned eleven when the Sino-Japanese war broke out. While tidings of hostilities kept filtering through, we at the home-front were not exactly out of harm's way. We, too, took a day at a time. Before every daybreak we would hear the resistance among us rise to their drills, yelling their lungs out: "Kill the foes! Kill the foes!" It at once exalted and tensed us. Then, at the cease of gunfire, kids in the neighborhood would emerge to count the dead – utterly unknowing of how things came to be. Not until the one night, that is, when I lay down among the bodies, held my breath, and feigned death to shake off the trailing enemies. It is but a matter of one breath between life and death! ... Or so realized the kid that I was then.

Reversal of Misfortune

The next year I left home to become a sramanera in Ch'i-hsia Shan. Training was in every way an ordeal. The greatest tribulation, however, was when, at fifteen, I humbly received the full ordination. The preceptor blew just a trifle too hard on the lit incense when he burned the twelve marks of precepts atop my crown, so much so they were caused to fuse. The top of my skull practically subsided. The anguish aside, parts of my brain were virtually scorched. And, in addition to considerable memory loss, my response was dulled in the process. But self-pity was never my way. Night after night, in reverence I invoked the name of the Buddha, and in earnestness I pleaded for the protection of Avalokitesvara Bodhisattva. I convalesced in time, my memory revived and intelligence much enhanced. So a misfortune brought along causes and conditions for fortune. In the reversal, my faith deepened.

In Sickness and, Again, in Sickness

That year I was seventeen. I was down with malaria, and the intermittent hot and cold bouts were insufferable. But then, all those of us who trained in the monasteries had begun on the resolve to entrust our physical body to the protection of the devas. Nobody, no matter what malady, would ever take a respite from work. So each day, I dragged my morbid self up and went about the routine like everyone else and, at the end of it, would slump lifelessly into the bed. A month had elapsed when, one day, Master Chih K'ai sent somebody to bring me a half-bowl of salted vegetables. Tearfully I held the bowl in both hands, thanked the master for his condescension, and vowed thus: "To repay my master, I, for as long as I shall live, offer my body and heart to Buddhism." Soon, strength returned to me and I was well again.

Two years later, I arrived at Chiao-shan Buddhist College to further my study. Not quite knowing why, I began to develop a heinous case of skin ulceration. For months I agonized without relief. Needless to say, the sores were purulent and scorching and, on those hot, sultry days, would glue to my garb.

In undressing to wash, they were torn again and again. The pain was excruciating beyond words! But, food in those destitute days was a problem enough, not to mention medication. My condition was never treated. Still – perhaps it was not meant to be that my life should end there – I made it over yet another hurdle.

Flights from Incarceration

I left Chiao-shan Buddhist College to assume the position of principal at Pai-t'a Primary School in Yihsing. The civil war in China was raging on. Not a day went past without either the armed nationalists or communists going about their manhunt. Many were seized and tortured, and too many died a wrongful death. The winds wept and the cranes wailed; and to the panic-stricken mind, a blade of grass or a bough from the tree would seem like the advancing foe. The rural scene, once so pure and tranquil, was mired in fearfulness and atrocity. Then one day, I was nabbed with the others. After ten days of incarceration, I found myself on the path to the execution ground. The world before me, I recall, was one stretch of yellowish gloom and murky desolation. It was not the fear of dying that took over my consciousness but a sense of pity: "What a shame that I am only twenty-one! Dreams and aspirations shall no longer be. Death is at hand. How life resembles the bubbles which are going to vanish without so much as a trace! The master, grandmother, and mother won't ever know ... " As the train of thoughts went on and on, someone, as if out of the blue, came up to me and led me away. Fear not in the face of death indeed! For fear would not at any time alleviate the circumstance.

Flight to Taiwan in 1949 with the monastic medical relief group led me into yet another incarceration. Rumors at the time were rampant that the communists were dispatching five hundred monastics to infiltrate Taiwan as agents. I along with Venerable Tz'ŭ Hang and some twenty other monastics from the mainland were locked up in a cell so jammed that we could not lie down but stood there for days and nights on end. All of us were tied and bound. No doubt that espionage was punishable by death under the circumstances but, in serenity, my mind remained quite free from delusion. I was prepared to affront the worst. Twenty-three days later, however, we were released – thanks to the endeavors of Wu Ching-hsiung, Sun-Chang Ching-yang, and others. Another passage through an aeon. Another rebirth. As emotions and thoughts brimmed over, my vow to preach the Dharma to benefit all sentient beings deepened.

Life, a Little Flawed

That year I took shelter in a monastery in Chungli. One day I was out on a rickety old bike. Suddenly, along the bumpy mountain path, two callow fellows came unknowingly toward me, at which I effected an intuitive swerve. The next instant, over the precipice man and bike plunged some forty feet below. When I came to, there I was, lying upside down, and my bike, literally all over the place. Swooning, I closed my eyes and told myself: "I'm a goner!"

After I knew not how long, I sat up, looked about, and began to wonder why the blossoms, the grass, the foliage, and the rocks in hell would seem so familiar. Would I be dead? Or alive? I touched my head, pinched myself, and did not honestly feel so *dead*. Then I felt my breath and the throb of my heart, and realized that, once again, I had made it through a catastrophic chapter in my life. I hurried on to retrieve the wreckage, bundled up the pieces, hauled them over my shoulder, and headed home – preoccupied with the ruin of the bike rather than my own safety. The day's entry in my journal was: "On better days, it's man on bike. Today, it's bike on man."

I was twenty-eight when I headed a traveling group to preach the Dharma across Taiwan and to raise funds for the copying of the Tripitaka. As a result of lugging a hefty projector all the way to the east, my legs became severely inflamed. The physician's prognosis at the time was amputation to curb the spreading condition. On that note, I, unfluttered, pondered to myself: "Thus inca- pacitated, I could well focus my energy on writing and other cultural endeavors." But while I channeled my efforts into seeking funds for the surgery, I also took time to heal pretty much on my own, and so my legs were spared. Little would I have envisaged, somehow, that the same pair of legs would be fractured forty years later from a fall in the bath. The very first thing I did, as I came to after the surgery, was to ask that my disciples in vigil outside be told this: "I feel just fine!" For two years thereafter I have continued to bustle about, cane in hand, preaching the Dharma. Life, a little flawed, is nonetheless positive!

Vihara in the Wind

In 1957, thanks to the devotees, I was given Universal Gate Vihara in Hsinpeitou for my residence. Once the typhoon struck and brought about a night's downpour. Then I heard rocks and earth come crashing down the slope at the back of the house. While in the pitch darkness I sat, composed and chanting the name of the Buddha, the storm raged like battling troops outside. Thus I heaved a sigh: "Should this place be wrecked in the havoc, I would forever be indebted to the graciousness of the devotees. Not only that, I sure would have a long way to go in cultivation to be worthy of such a nice abode." The morning after, at the cease of the storm, I stepped outside to inspect the damages. Lo and behold! While the lower portion of the hillside caved in completely, the upper portion – which hung over the vihara – remained absolutely intact. Amidst it all, the vihara was as good as it ever was! As witnesses of the wonder sweated on my behalf, I silently thanked all the Buddhas and Bodhisattvas for delivering me from the mortal perils.

In l981 I fell ill again. This time, the acute back pain that I had was diagnosed as fatal. The physicians at Taiwan Veterans General Hospital, after scrutinizing my X-ray films, decided that I had but two more months left of this life. They then exhorted me to return within days for another examination. Inundated as I always was with work, I simply failed to do as told. Exactly a year later, when I made it back for the long overdue examination, my doctor, visibly stunned, took a long, long while before he could phrase himself, asking: "Did you at any time hurt your back?" That surely picked my brain. Then I recalled what did happen ages ago. I was out surveying the aftermath of another typhoon and, in so doing, took a bad fall. The incident eluded me completely for, as always, life was too onerous to keep check of myself. So it finally dawned on everybody that the black spot caught on film was the hematoma from way back!

Successors I Have a Few

In 1964 we invited layman[1] Li Chüeh-ho, father of Reverend Tzu Chuang and then executive officer of the chanting group in Ilan, to give us a hand in the launching of Shou-shan Temple in Kaohsiung. Within days he took sick and was subsequently diagnosed as having suffered diverse illnesses for some years. It was a marvel to follow his life from that point on. For another twenty years he toiled on, took his renunciation with me at age seventy-five, and relinquished his longevity for a future life at the ripe old age of eighty.

A few among the younger generations of disciples, too, were celebrated for their dauntlessness in the face of the most vicious

---

[1] A householder who practices Buddhism at home without becoming a monastic.

physical inflictions. Reverend Yung Wen was barely twenty when she began her academic pursuits in America. Hailed the *Super Nun* by teachers and peers, she graduated with distinction despite devastations from lupus erythematosus. Never had her optimism and laboriousness waned throughout her battle. She now heads Buddha's Light Hsi Lai School. Reverend Yi Kuan was almost buried alive in a horrendous landslide while supervising the construction of Chi-lo Temple; and Reverend Yung Man was bashed in the head in a mayhem, standing guard in the parking lot of Fo Kuang Shan, when a treacherous mob struck. None of them ever let out as much as a moan or cower before suffering. I cannot describe my joyful appreciation of their dedication to the Dharma and selflessness in serving the masses.

To Live and Die on One's Own

Let me close with some records of the effortlessness and compliance with which the eminent masters of the past received their end. Ch'an Master Liang Chieh of Tung Shan entered extinction in a sitting position after he had lectured to the congregation. But on hearing his wailing disciples, he opened his eyes and resurrected. Seven days later, after discoursing to disciples on the abstinence from ignorance, he again sat in an upright position and relinquished his life. Ch'an Master Tê P'u ordered the preparation of a vegetarian feast as offering in worship, which he heartily consumed. In equanimity, then, he passed on. Ch'an Master Hsing K'ung of the Chin dynasty [265-420] charged into the camp of the rebelling Hsü Ming and rebuked him for wreaking carnage on the innocents. The rebels, infuriated, were about to slay the master when he started to chant a verse and then proclaimed himself the *Merry Martyr*. This averted the animosity of the rebels, who turned around to escort him home, thus sparing the indigenous residents and their properties. Later, Master Hsing K'ung, realizing the approach of his end, seated himself in a self-built wooden barrel and sailed down the river. He played his flute as he followed the flow, and passed away. Three days thereafter, the master was found in the same sitting position on the beachfront. Many other prodigious cases certainly existed. Ch'an Master Tan Hsia passed away in an upright standing position – pole in hand and wearing his shoes. The living Buddha of Chin Shan, Miao Ch'an, quietly passed away amidst a shower – also standing. Ch'an Master Yin Fêng passed away standing, too, on his head. Layman P'ang Yün and his family also lived and died in accordance with their integrity. These ancestral sages of the Ch'an school, coming and going in ease as they did, had every intention of revealing to the laity this:

> Let go of the grapple,
> Flow with the conditioning causes,
> Open up the mind –
> Transcension over and beyond
>   life and death
> One shall find.

"The impartial mind[2] is the way." The cycle of life and death is really the natural course of the changes and operations between heaven and earth. Hence death, no more than the quitting of one body for another, must be viewed with the impartial mind. For it is the

---

[2] Literally, ordinary mind. Nondiscriminatory mind.

consciousness (similar to what is known as the *code of life*) and the strength of karma which will, without cessation, be transferred from one life to the next. Therefore, life is not real living; nor is death real dying. On that note, why fear life and death? Instead, let us, with a grip of what is before us, continue to create all the lives to come. That is of the essence!

AS MY VOW
SUBLIMED

皆

大

歡

喜

Raised in a Buddhist family, I vehemently asked to be allowed to become fully vegetarian at the early age of four. Then, the most natural causes and conditions impinged upon my worldly life, which I renounced – at age twelve – for the monastery.

Before turning twenty, however, I did what most other devotees would do. Amidst the wafting incense in the grandeur of the shrine, I prostrated and faithfully said my prayers to the Buddhas and Bodhisattvas: O The great Buddha! The most compassionate Avalokitesvara Bodhisattva! Please strengthen and support me, and bestow upon me intelligence, wisdom, courage, and vigor. Pray, let the path before me be smooth.

Daily, after morning and evening services, the same plea was repeated. I was certain that was the way I should pray.

Then, at turning twenty, a thought flashed through my mind: Were I being self-serving asking this and that of the Buddha each day the way I had been carrying on? Should all Buddhists be as insatiable as I had been, wouldn't the Buddhas and Bodhisattvas be absolutely aggrieved!

From that point on until I reached age forty, the content of my prayer had indeed undergone certain changes. At the full completion of services of merit, worship, chanting, and preaching, I prayed: O The great Buddha! The most compassionate Avalokitesvara Bodhisattva! Please strengthen and support my parents, teachers, relatives, and friends, and all protectors of and devotees in the Dharma. Pray, let them be healthy, their paths be smooth, and their families be secure!

The Buddha lowered his eyes and smiled, as if commending my progress. I, too, was at peace – a trifle delighted even – with myself for having realized the need to pray for others instead of myself.

On reaching age forty, again I reflected and introspected, and this I came to clinch: I was still praying daily for the interest of the self and not in complete accord with the Dharma! For all those I had asked to be protected and blessed were affiliated to *myself*, and my prayer had remained a form of selfish desire.

From ages forty to sixty, in particular, my prayer appeared to be going through a

metamorphosis. It went: O The great Buddha!
The most compassionate Avalokitesvara
Bodhisattva! Pray, let there be peace in the
world and harmony among humankind, and
let the causes and conditions be delivered[1] for
all beings.

Recitation of this passage would invariably render me brimming with the joy of the
Dharma. I even professed to have taken a
remarkable stride in practice and, no longer
praying on my own behalf or for the weal of
those dear to me, to be living the words of
Avataṃsaka[2] *Sutra*:

> [I] only pray that all beings be delivered
> from suffering, and ask not that peace and
> contentment be mine.

My perception kept on evolving in the
course of time. Sixty years went by, and it
dawned on the field of my eighth consciousness that I had let the Buddhas and
Bodhisattvas down. Why did I always have to

[1] Literally, to be transported across the river of trans-
migration.
[2] Garland. The sutra is the foundation text of the Hua-yen
school.

ask them to do this and that for me? So what had I done so far? In the stillness of the night I contemplated. How could I help being ashamed!

Here I am approaching seventy, in this manner I now pray without cease: O The great Buddha! The most compassionate Avalokitesvara Bodhisattva! Pray, let me take over the karmic hindrances, sufferings, and plights of all beings! Pray, let me bear the bitterness of life in this world! Pray, let me carry on and effect the benevolence and sympathy of the Buddha! Pray, let me take my place beside you to instruct all beings and to bless them with joy!

As my mind sublimates, the scope of my life keeps broadening with each horizon and reaching for new heights. In the daily prayer I seem to have picked my way through the spring, summer, fall, and winter of life. On a singular vow I have expended more than sixty years before gradually attaining to a little revelation such as this. Cultivation is certainly a long and winding road!

HAPPILY EVER AFTER

Once Su Tung-po and Ch'in Shao-yu[1] were heatedly debating on the origin of a flea. Ch'an Master Fo Yin, commenting on the confrontation, wrote this verse:

> The vernal breeze through a tree takes
> two courses,
> Warming the southern bough while
> chilling the north;
> Here it is, a notion from the west,
> A bit of which flashes westward and
> a bit east.

The poem is among my personal favorites for its sense of universal happiness. For the longest time I had recited it often. Then came this revelation: In being myself and coping with matters, I do aspire after happiness for all.

Innate Happiness

The disposition to ensure everybody be happy first evidenced in me as a tot of three. Poor though we were, I would not think twice before hastening to share with playmates a

[1] Both celebrated T'ang poets.

slice of cake obtained from the Buddha's shrine or an unusual pebble spotted by the roadside as if it were some incomparable gem. On festive occasions, I would drag with all my might the family candy-can out to the front yard and give my buddies a hearty treat. In the end neighbors would tease my mother for raising a foolhardy kid. As for me, I honestly had not an inkling how hard livelihood was for the older folks then. I just felt great at the sight of everyone having a great time. So I never quite tired of my doings, and mockery never quite dampened my spirits.

At age twelve I left home to become a monastic and entered a life completely apart from the worldly ways. Nonetheless I continued to seek happiness for all in whatever I did. As I basked in the teachings of the Dharma, I was enabled to make cross-references between comprehension and practice. I gradually awakened to the fact that compassion and generosity, kindly words and supportive actions in the Buddhist doctrine are indeed meant to ensure all shall fare happily ever after.

Throughout my career both as a student and a speaker of the Dharma, I would make every effort to ensure well-being be shared among all, good news be available to everyone, all distress be relieved, while burdens and sufferings be mine. The menial person that I was at the monastery when I newly arrived in Taiwan in 1949 would strive to make time to read and write out of an enormous workload. Then I realized those around were not exactly agreeable to my scholarly pursuits. So I rescheduled myself to work in the day and study at night. Diligently I acquired the native dialect, which soon enabled me to communicate freely with others and to interpret the abbot's lectures for diverse audiences. All that was well did end well.

Bridge Across Generation Gaps

The innovative approach I adopted as I spoke in Ilan during 1952 drew quite a group of young devotees whose vivacity alienated some of the older monastics. Taking it upon myself to bridge this gap between the generations, young and old were coping happily ever after. Even now, Reverends Tzu Chuang, Hsin Ping, Tzu Hui, Tzu Jung, Tzu

Chia, and others still savor the memory of the way Ai-ku used to bring me a bowl of plain noodles, insisting that no one should touch it, and how I would wait until she was gone to share it with everybody. There is no turning back in time, but the feel of joy from the past shall always be. Not only that, but forever I shall ensure happiness be unto all. If on occasion I should be the only one given a bowl of rice while no other was, or noodles be cooked expressly for me after the departure of guests, I would honestly be very displeased.

I would treat the youngest and most junior coming to hear me speak as best I could. I would just as well invite them to have tea and dine with me or to go sightseeing together. At times guests were a trifle hesitant in responding and, anxious on my behalf, disciples waiting by would attempt to intervene. But no embarrassment would suffice to curb me. All that I would want was that everybody be happy. Hence nicknamed the *Reverse Vehicle of Compassion*, I in utter humility could only pledge to emulate Avalokitesvara Bodhisattva in relieving all living beings of their suffering and bringing joy to all.

In matters of transportation, I would always opt for as accommodating a vehicle as we could afford. Lately I am journeying about in a minivan for nine. That way we can all travel together in ease and with pleasure. Once on an annual tour to the branch temples with the graduating class of the Buddhist college, I had such fun that I literally took turn to ride in each of the four buses just so that I could spend time with everybody. At times the disciples' concern that I might be overly fatigued would become quite vocal. But, reticently appreciative of advice that was really contrary to my nature, I could not comply.

The sights and sounds and souvenirs along my many travels I could not wait to share with disciples and devotees on my return. I would want everyone to come away with something each time. That is the gist of happiness for all.

Joy be unto the World

With early activities concentrated in Ilan, northern Taiwan, devotees in the south also started voicing their demands. Next came years of tireless commuting. Ultimately, Fo Kuang Shan sparked the coming of a multitude of branch temples across Taiwan and around the globe, each for the benefit and to the content of devotees there. Many would wonder about these mammoth undertakings and the astronomical costs they must have entailed. In essence, fundraising was conducted locally such that everyone would share in the joy of giving.

Those of us at Fo Kuang Shan believe in "accommodating the aged, employing the strong, and rearing the young." To fare happily ever after, tire not in the quest for the position and practice that pertain to our own nature. Each of us is the embodiment of the spirit of humanistic Buddhism. What better manifests the grand cause of spreading the Dharma to benefit all living beings than such a realization!

Harmony be Among Us

Not counting the countless devotees, I must have gained over a thousand disciples in all. They are of all ages and come from diverse milieus, and no one shares the same disposition or thinking. The only key to harmony is let them live happily ever after! At each year's personnel rotation and placement, I would make a point of interviewing all the graduates and interns from the Buddhist college, enquire about their aspirations, strengths, studies, and even family concerns, and advise them accordingly. In the process, I ensure the annual reshuffling be completed with joy.

Generation gaps are practically nonexistent at Fo Kuang Shan. For close to three decades an atmospheric harmony prevails. This absence of querulousness must have a lot to do with my innate joy. Matters which disciples have finalized I rarely overturn; affairs unreported to me I leave to the hands of others; blunders I fix alongside those in charge; slips of the tongue I can harbor well – perhaps with a dash of humor – hoping a lesson is ultimately learned somewhere.

In the same token, those of us at Fo Kuang Shan are always in touch with others around us, financing public utilities and helping improve living conditions, establishing schools and classes for the young, celebrating festivities with the masses, and giving to the needy – just so that we shall all live happily ever after.

Peace be unto Society

In 1990, Xu Jiatun, then head of the Hong Kong branch office of New China News Agency, got in touch with me on his arrival in the United States. The two of us did hail from the same hometown in China, and I wanted to ensure he would be welcome to return someday. Moreover, neither country should in any way be abashed because of his leaving. So I received him, and he and all parties concerned fared happily thereafter.

Last March, Taiwan was virtually shaken by the brawl over a statue of Avalokitesvara Bodhisattva in a public park in downtown Taipei. The ensuing gridlock seemed to last forever. "If it were not I who must tread the hells, who would that be?"[2] I began to lobby the Buddhist and Christian circles and the mayor's office and in the end came up with a solution that would please

---

[2] The vow of Ksitigarbha Bodhisattva, the deliverer from the hells.

everyone. The Buddhists kept their statue and the authorities their dignity, and the Christians were projected in the most virtuous light. When asked later how I brought about the joyous grand finale, my response was that I had hoped for one from the very start.

Too many times had I been the peacemaker among contentious politicians, between the polarized authorities and masses, among feuding governing bodies, and between rival public figures. I remember years ago the lifting of the martial law in Taiwan was, oddly enough, followed by massive labor dispute. That day, I summoned a general meeting of the entire 600-member staff and asked if anyone intended to join the demonstration demanding a raise. On top of that, I asked if everyone was coping. I must say I was quite taken aback on hearing the consensus: "We don't need a raise. At Fo Kuang Shan we have faith, and we have incomparable joy!" How well put!

Certainly there are good days and bad days. At times the intention to bring happiness to all simply does not prevail. The elderly folks at the homes cannot share the same appetite and tastes; many young men and women cannot find the opportunity to become monastics when they ask to; and far too many wishes still wait to be accommodated.

Once some scholar called democracy and science the two pivotal factors in social progress. But take a look at the state of affairs Taiwan is in. Competition is brutal, whether in political elections or school examinations; standards do not seem to exist, whether in government measures or corporate policies. If practicing democracy and progressive science and technology fail to bring about the sense of joy and blessedness, they in time shall fail. Talk of unification is certainly in the air. But take caution that unification would only mean something when both parties should approach the issue with full intention of seeking to be together happily ever after.

IN A MOMENT'S KṢAṆA

Known these days as the *Great Limit of 1997*, the prospect of returning Hong Kong to China is strumming the pain of many who call the place home. During my first lecture tour there in 1990, I was bombarded with questions on what I thought would lie ahead.

"All is within a moment's *kṣaṇa*,"[1] I replied.

The so-called principle of the opposing base and point in the meditative method has never stopped reverberating in my mind through experiences of all forms – be them under the fumigation of the Dharma at the ancient monasteries in the depth of the mountains as a young novice, or in the act of spreading the Dharma to benefit all sentient beings as a full-fledged monastic. The potentialities, conditions, opportunities, and encounters we speak of in this world, I find, do transpire in a moment's *kṣaṇa*.

At leisure, I would – book in hand – allow myself to ramble between heaven and earth in spirit. Records, past and present, at home and abroad, are rife with reversals of

---

[1] Sanskrit for a thought or the time of a thought.

defeat and loss in conflicts and ventures, all of which having hinged on a moment's kṣaṇa. A recent read of *Li Teng-hui tê yi-ch'ien t'ien* (The Thousand Days of Li Teng-hui) and Hao Po-ts'un's *Wu K'uei* (Guiltless) doubly verifies my point. Every move – be it in the web of interrelationships among us or in the making of policies that are sure to impact on our lives – is decided, I find, within a moment's kṣaṇa.

Forever an observer, researcher, and analyst of the multifarious ways of this world, their beginning and end, and their ultimate, I have never ceased to recognize how closely the successes and failures, gains and losses, and conditions ebbing and flowing in the span of our life have banked on the kṣaṇa of a moment. Many, many decisions down the vista of my past, indeed, were such formulations.

Immersing in the Ocean of the Dharma

That year I turned eleven. My mother and I left home to look for my father who was missing in the war. Passing by the monastery at Ch'i-hsia Shan, my mother paused to pay tribute to the Buddha. While she prayed, I roamed about, poking my nose here and there. Then, the venerable who was the receptionist came by and, as if out of the blue, put the question before me: "Little fellow, would you want to be a monastic?" I, anxious to get back to my mother, replied in accordance with what arose in my mind: "Well, yes!" At that he escorted me to the presence of Master Chih K'ai (who did become my master). As the dire train of events continued to unfold, I kept my word and bade my mother farewell. For this casual singular kṣaṇa I have every appreciation to this very day. It launched me early into the infinite ocean of Truth and the savor of the Dharma.

While many fled the country at the takeover of China in 1949 by the communist regime, I readied myself to stay with Hua-ts'ang Temple whether for weal or woe. In the nick of time, however, fellow monastic Venerable Chih Yung rescinded his plan and entrusted me with the leadership of the monastic medical relief group that he had organized. Thus, at the kṣaṇa of the moment, I, for the good of all, took the group across the strait to Taiwan, leaving behind my old home and loved ones. The same change of mind had since hastened the continuation of my efforts in the Buddhist wisdom. But, never have I forgotten the gift of my mother and the teaching of my master; nor has my diligence to preach the Dharma for the benefit of all sentient beings ever slackened. I pray that these efforts would bring consolation – if only the slightest – to those so dear to me.

Joining the Crowd

Very shy by nature, I used to be petrified by the idea of having to face the crowd. How I relished the anonymity of those early years in Taiwan, undertaking all the menial tasks while writing to spread the Dharma!

I ran into layman Li Chüeh-ho at Lungshan Temple in March, 1952. He was in the midst of a baffling search for monastics willing to preach in Ilan, which was deemed too remote for most. In sympathy I volunteered my service. Li was elated and, in no time, an official appointment letter found its way to me. So it was on wings of a thought of sympathy that I came upon the placid plain of

Ilan. And it was at the impetus of the same thought of kindness that I came to take confidence in administering the rain of the Dharma to irrigate the minds of all living beings. The journey to Ilan, indeed, was the most monumental turning point in my entire life.

As self-confidence before the congregation grew, so did the invitations to preach. I began to pick my way up the mountains and down to the waterfront. Then, devotees from as far as Kaohsiung came to seek the Dharma. As feverish as the sun over southern Taiwan, their welcome would render me extremely ill at ease: the band at the train station, the parade through the heart of town, the cacophony of firecrackers and applause, the curious stare of passers-by, and the public commotion that seemed to drag on forever. A few times I had hopped onto a different train, trying to dodge attention, but in vain.

Once I went to enquire after the condition of a devotee in sickness – only to discover a massive gathering of devotees from nearby waiting to invite me into their homes, which I did as best I could for all my life I would make it a point to comply to every good wish coming my way. At the end of a day's home visits and sumptuous treats, I was worn – and full – beyond words. Zealous and reverent as the devotees of Kaohsiung were, the slightness of my own blessedness and virtue did at that point make me think twice: truly I was unworthy of the sustenance lavished upon me. This gave rise to the notion of not returning to Kaohsiung thereafter. But, when the train was about to depart, Wêng-Ch'en P'ên, an amicable elderly lady, came rushing up to my carriage, and she said to me: "Master, you must come back!" I knew not how many people had given me that same line, or for how many times in all, but the pining in her voice and heartiness in her countenance struck a chord within me. Touched by the instant, I was determined to uphold the Dharma cause[2] that bound me to Kaohsiung. There and then, indeed, was sown the seed of Fo Kuang Shan.

Affirming the Sangha Character

Mayor Ch'en Wu-chang of Kaohsiung had

---

[2] The sense of universal altruism giving rise to compassion.

every intention to hand over to me Chung-lieh Tz'ŭ (Shrine for the Loyal and Valiant) in Shou-shan Park to be renovated into a Buddhist temple. The only condition was that the original name of Chung-lieh Tz'ŭ be kept. For the next instant, I found myself mulling over one question: How would I, who have all my life donned the patched garment of a Buddhist monk, justifiably go and head an ancestral shrine? So, for the purpose of clarity, I put forth the revised title of Chung-lieh Ssŭ (Temple). It was met with negation. At that, I, too, called it quits. A few were saddened on my behalf for what they regarded to be a propitious course gone askew, but many more, witnessing the working of my kṣaṇa, became much reaffirmed in their reverence for the sanctitude of the sangha character.

Later on, the devotees of Kaohsiung undertook to acquire the site where Shou-shan Temple and its Buddhist college now perch. The rapid expansion which ensued would call for another temple to be put up elsewhere. At the time, a scenic plot by Cheng Ching Lake (Clear and Pure Lake) caught our eyes but, just as a deposit was to be offered, a disciple was heard exclaiming excitedly:

"With our temple by the lake, President Chiang[3] could conveniently drop by to pray to the Buddha while vacationing out there!" I could not have disagreed more. For the presence of a temple and the sangha would be for the benefit of the masses, who could come purposely to hear the Dharma and practice, and certainly not just to drive through the premises and admire the view! So, how could we foolishly think of basking ourselves in the reflections upon a lake instead of in the glory of the Buddha?

Thus a moment's kṣaṇa had awakened me to the relinquishment of the splendid Cheng Ching Lake. Regrets I had none whatsoever. And those who cried shame had all reverted to agreeing to the decisiveness and prudence that I exercised. For the coming of Fo Kuang Shan later was the true fruition of the collaborative endeavors of the sangha and devotees. And, as we would come to see, the spiritual mountain and sacred land which we opened with bare hands, too, did take form in a moment's kṣaṇa. How inscrutable!

[3] Chiang Kai-shek.

The Coming of Fo Kuang Shan

Some time in 1967, quite fortuitously I was told of a financially smitten Chinese family from Vietnam by the name of Ch'u. So dire were their circumstances that they were on the brink of total despair, even suicide. To give them a hand, I immediately resorted to raising funds for the purchase of the mountain property under their name. But for one brief compassionate moment's kṣaṇa, I found myself up against the consensus because the property, neither scenic nor accessible, was but a wretched wilderness of thickets and weeds.

Tough enough it was to dissuade everyone around, and infinitely tougher was the travail itself. In the long, hard days that followed, we toiled under the torrid sun, virtually moving mountain, or amidst frenzied hurricanes, blocking waters. The prosperity of Fo Kuang Shan before our eyes is the reward of twenty-eight years of excavation in labor as much as in wisdom. True, therefore, that a kṣaṇa would suffice to create a turning point in life but, more important, we must all aspire to and persevere in the fulfillment of that one kṣaṇa providing the impetus.

One kṣaṇa after another had transported me from home to monastery, from the mainland to Taiwan, from Ilan to Kaohsiung, from Shou-shan Temple to Fo Kuang Shan, and eventually around the globe. Be it a casual, chivalrous, fervent, or compassionate kṣaṇa, I am perfectly willing to uphold it, perfect it, and suffer for it.

Outset of the Constant Mind[4]

The dilapidated state in which I found of the Buddhist affairs in Taiwan when I came shattered me. Thoughts of how we could break ourselves through kept invading me until, one day, there arose visions of an exhibition hall and a library. Though armed with little else than an imperishable mind of the constant, I set out to make the kṣaṇa a reality. Every dollar on me would be channeled toward the purchase of books; on every journey I would take time to acquire select Buddhist relics. Today, virtually every

---

[4] Perseverance.

Buddhist college or branch temple houses a library or exhibition hall – the living proof of the fortitude which is the facilitating condition in the maturation of an effort and the fulfillment of a cause.

One way or another I have remained gravely concerned with the directions and prospects of the Buddhist faith. Once – it must have been some thirty years ago – the engrossed essayist that I was, under the question *What needs Buddhism*, put down the following: a university, a newspaper, and a radio and television station. When tabled before others later, these proposals were somehow met with disdain and labeled an absurdity. True that for want of causes and conditions, the shortlist is yet to be realized in full. But the kṣaṇa is as good as it was at its inception decades back.

The coming of Hsi Lai University in Los Angeles in 1990 and that of Fo Kuang University in Ilan in 1993 were only the beginning. In time other institutions will go up for the benefit of all. And our young shall be taught the Dharma, coached in practice, and infused with compassion and wisdom. In time, too, the newspaper and broadcasting station will go up, as thoughts of them have never ceased to prompt me.

I must mention the occasion of a Sino-Thai Buddhist conference that I attended a long, long time ago. Before we knew it, I remember, communication screeched to a deadlock over sundry matters. Halfway through I was compelled to rise and draw the attention to three emergencies: solidarity, unification, and mobilization. A kṣaṇa turned the tide, and the event proceeded in friendly discussions of the three issues. Recollections of that day did return from time to time for, after all, it manifested the resolve of a moment, which I uphold in all my endeavors. Like Ch'an Master Hui T'ung, who was enlightened from a feather in hand, and Chih Hsien of Hsiangyen, who came to see his own nature from hitting a rock, the rise of a kṣaṇa may seem sudden but really is not. That one moment is the culmination of years and years of committed practice!

Widening of Heaven and Earth

To the good I would adhere with deter-mination and vest my life in its realization, but, at the recognition of a word of gentility, I would be equally prepared to comply, turn my head, and change my mind.

In 1957, on being admitted as a doctoral candidate at Taishō University in Japan, I was busying myself in preparations for the journey. At some point, layman Chu Tien-yüan said to me: "Master! Why do you need a degree when in our heart you are a teacher above any other?" How his words rendered me perspiring with embarrassment! Long had I relinquished the worldly life for the extraordinary mission of spreading the Dharma to purify the mind of all sentient beings, how could I, master to my disciples and followers, be so obsessed with personal interests and justifiably abandon them to seek tuition from the masters in Japan? So, in a moment's kṣaṇa, plans of further studies were dropped for good. The reward was a fuller, more meaningful life thereafter as I turned to concentrate my energies into the benefit of others.

My disciple Reverend Man Ho, a distinguished English graduate from National Taiwan University, was about to launch out on her ever-promising scholarly pursuits in the United States when, in her soul-searching, she wrote me thus:

> It is from resolve and compassion, not erudition, that the cultivation of a monastic begins. I was driven in the direction of the academia by aspirations and urging not my own. No, it is none of these that I want. For I am here to renounce the worldly ways.

Precisely in a moment's kṣaṇa she and postgraduate education passed each other by. She is now in charge of sundry undertakings: academic affairs at Hsi Lai University, editorial of *Hsi Lai News*, simultaneous interpretation for my lectures, and translation of my speeches. All of these she has tackled with marked competence and with the joy of the Dharma. I have every reason to believe that she and I share in the same thankfulness for that moment's kṣaṇa.

Blossoms Falling, Lotus Rising

T'ien Jan of Tanhsia was about to set out on a trip to the capital for the official examination when he heard someone pop the question:

"In the choice [of a career], how could officialdom be the same as Buddhahood?" So, at the kṣaṇa of the moment, he laid down all aspirations for fame and fortune, and headed toward Hunan. On reaching the gate of Hsi Ch'ien of Shiht'ou, he stayed to study and, eventually, attained to enlightenment. The sixth Ch'an patriarch Hui Neng was a woodcutter who, at the prodding of An Tao-ch'êng, seized the kṣaṇa of the moment and relinquished the worldly life. He made it all the way to Huangmei where, under the fifth Ch'an patriarch Hung Jên, he became enlightened and saw his own nature.

Though short on talents, I did on a few occasions show disciples and devotees the way with a word, a line, or a kṣaṇa. Among them, Chang Tz'ŭ-lien, at my exhortation, gave up dreams of a singing career to become a Buddhist dedicated to child education – the raising of the Bodhi buds. What merits! Reverend Yi Chao had reversed her ambition in Taiwanese operetta-singing to take the tonsure. She has since undertaken key positions in various branch temples and is presently heading the vihara in Paris – converting many in her turn.

The sutra states: "The heart, like a master painter, is capable of painting diverse worlds." There in a moment's kṣaṇa exists heaven and hell, joy and sorrow, birth, aging, sickness, and death. But the reception of my share of hindrances and hurt is – without fail – full of good spirits, which always ferry me across the worst of woes.

Self-existing in Life and Death

Too many kalpas have I been through, and a few times was I verging on death! Neither fear nor ecstasy did overcome me. I would think that between life and death lies but the kṣaṇa of a moment. If in life, time and space were maneuverable to the benefit of others, how should the end be feared? For in leaving a legacy, we live after death. Reversely, for those of us who should expend our life in evil, no bunker or elixir would suffice to shield us from or cure us of fear of all forms, and living would be worse than dying. A life squandered in merriment and idleness, I would even say, is as good as death.

Verily, I know not what to say to the

media in reply to their questions about the fate of Hong Kong because I know not a thing about politics or economy. All that I can comprehend of the worldly ways pertain to causes and conditions, rewards and retributions – all of them often hanging on the kṣaṇa of a moment.

"A slip of the foot leads to the regret of eternity, and, turning back, a hundred years have gone past." "At the flare of anger, a million hindrances are seen to fling open their gates." "On one call of the name of the Buddha, Buddhahood is attained by all." We know too well what each of these means. Be it greed, anger, stupidity, ignorance, evil, prejudice, egotism, or pride, the slightest kṣaṇa of a moment can damage the mind sufficiently to bring about grave consequences. But in timely repentance – with palms closed and reflections heartiest – the kṣaṇa of the moment can bring about the most wondrous splendor!

"In a kṣaṇa lies the great chiliocosm of three kinds of thousands of chiliocosms." The thought of a moment impacts on our own life as much as the lives of others. Let us, therefore, be circumspect in each kṣaṇa, reflect and introspect at the rise of every, and ensure that it abides safely in compassion, prajna, the weal of all sentient beings, and the Dharma!

I'LL BE YOUR PRIDE

T he loss of my father further sank an already plighted family in the behold of neighbors. He vanished on his return from business in Hangchou and was presumed to have perished in gunfire. The Japanese had then launched assault on northern China. The year was 1937. My widowed mother was not one to be overtaken by self-pity, however. In the firmest tone she told her four young ones: "No need to be vexed, my children. Just strive on and excel!"

At her words, I was prepared to charge ahead in life.

Mother, I'll be Your Pride

Economy at home, as underdeveloped as it was then, required that we cross the canal by boat to make purchases on the other bank. But during the Sino-Japanese war, no one would risk boating across for ten or twenty cents. On seeing this, I, then but ten, would gallantly volunteer my service. I would strip to my waist, tie my shirt round my forehead, and plunge right into the rapids below. In no time I would return with everything everybody had shortlisted. The villagers, giving me the thumbs-up, would exclaim: "That second brother from the Li family sure is something!" Realization of the unmistakable pride in my mother's smile reassured me thus: "I'm going to be better still!"

The year after, I escorted my fragile mother to go in quest of my father. Leaving home, we chanced to pass by Ch'i-hsia Temple. Under the most incidental conditions, I gave the abbot my word to receive the tonsure and to renounce the worldly life. Mother, swallowing back her tears, saw my determination and was compelled to turn back alone. I watched her solitary figure disappearing in the distance and cried inside: "Mother, don't worry. I'll be your pride!"

The unknowing sramanera that I was when I first trained at the monastery was a popular subject of jokes for those around me. Each time my mother's words would return to me: "Strive on and excel!" So I worked all the harder, vowed to be diligent, and in the end did earn the recognition that was due me.

Just as unforgettable was how I groped

my way through writing endeavors. Once composing on *Uncovering the Prajna by Way of Nonattachment to the Bodhi*, a topic about which I had problem even reading, I did whatever I could and submitted quite a few pages. This poem came back from the teacher: "In the jade-green willows two gold orioles twitter, / Up the azure above a flock of white egrets soar." It brought a hearty laugh among my peers, who interpreted for me: "What the teacher meant was, whatever you were trying to say eluded him completely!"

The next time around, we were to write on *My Hometown*. I pondered long and plotted hard, and read my essay through and through. It would be my best-ever work, I was content to think. A few days later, another poem came back: "Like counting jewels not your own, / Not a fraction of them you own."

The first time it was unreadable, and this time, allegedly plagiaristic. Still, it did not irk me. Nor did I lose steam. I became exceedingly observant and discerning. In time, my writings became more polished and they gradually earned the recognition they deserved both in class and in the local papers. Honestly, it is up to us to find ways to break ourselves through bafflement and wrong so as to get ahead.

Audacity Inspires

Being Master Chih K'ai's only disciple was perhaps why he was tougher with me than with the others. Once I was scathed by another teacher and the master, on learning about it, sent for me. After giving me plentiful advice, he asked if I was coping. With little hesitation, I began relating to him the impoverished state that I was in, wanting in everything from clothes to stationeries. But, instead of commiserating with me, he picked up a cup of tea from the table before him and said to me: "Do you think that, in having little means, you are going to get anything from me? Let me get this straight: I might just as well save my tea money and you would find it much, much more than you could have needed. Still, I would not spare you anything. Why, I am not going to tell you now; you shall have no problem finding out for yourself."

Another time, while studying at Chiao-shan Buddhist College, I was down with an excruciating case of skin ulceration. With no means for treatment, I in desperation wrote to report my condition to the master. His reply, to my utter shock, began thus: "That self-pitying note of yours has just reached me ... "

Admittedly, I did feel wronged some-what. But thereafter I came to realize how very much my master cared. Had he patron-ized me, consoled me, or supported me to make life easier for me, I would have been glad and so would he. But, in reversing his way, he would want me to train in fortitude, ride the most grinding times, and excel!

On the publication of *Shih-chia-mou-ni Fo ch'uan* (Biography of Sakyamuni Buddha) in 1955, the first thought that came to mind was to present a copy to my master. A copy did make it back to the mainland, which was held incommunicado at the time, and was I thrilled to hear from him! The urge to reach him was really to let him know that this disciple would never let him down!

Thereafter we lost touch again. Another forty years had marched on. I was not able to return home until 1989 – only to find that the master had died in the Cultural Revolution.

Upon his grave, I was absolutely beside

myself with grief. Tears pouring and heart stricken, there I told him: "I've made it home!" His face I might never see again or his pride I might never be, but I had pleaded that his honor be redeemed and his family be cared for. And, though late but not never, I have also taken upon myself to tend to their needs as his disciple should.

Vow to Open the Universal Gate

In 1949 I arrived at Shan-tao Temple to see fifteen or sixteen people around a dinner table for eight. Knowingly, I left in silence.

With nowhere else to turn to, I thought of looking up an old classmate at a monastery somewhere in Keelung. By the time my two companions and I dragged our jaded selves through the bitter cold and sad drizzle and reached the mountain gate, it was already one in the afternoon. Those from the monastery, on hearing that we had been famished for a whole day, were about to escort us into the kitchen when someone said aloud: "One of the senior venerables has specifically instructed that, in light of our own meager circumstances, they be asked to seek help elsewhere please!" As I turned to depart, my old friend motioned me to hold. He then hastened to buy two catties of rice on his own and cooked us a pot of congee. I would never, ever forget holding the bowl with hands that were quivering from hunger. At the end of the meal, we thanked him and, through the same bitter cold and sad drizzle, once again took the road to the unknown.

The experience had carved so deeply into my bones and heart that I came to vow thus: I will let the *p'u-mên* (universal gate) be open at all times to receive whoever approaches. Two decades since, P'u-mên Ching-shê (Vihara) and P'u-mên Temple were erected in Taipei for the kindly reception of devotees from all over. And, as a rule, Fo Kuang Shan's branch temples will always have two extra meal tables ready for unexpected guests, and travel funds be offered to wandering monastics. The offering of clear tea and light meals to others today may be but a cup of water to a cart of burning wood, but I believe sincerity is the most invaluable gem of all.

The high school, kindergarten, and even journal of Fo Kuang Shan were all named Universal Gate. It means the appearance of the Buddhas and Bodhisattvas therein. I hope that we shall emulate the spirit of the Buddhas and Bodhisattvas in receiving all the living beings.

Often reflecting in the still of the night on events and people from the past, I could not help feeling for those peers who had succumbed to the adversities of livelihood and pressures from opinion. Many of them either left or ended in ruins.

Hence I believe that in excelling, we are not battling out of a moment's mere impulses but for the great endeavors of all time, and in striving ahead, we are not after personal good but the weal and blessings of all living beings.

Thoughts of this commitment in my faith and to my devotees would, time and again, impinge upon the serenity of my mind like waves. I have never bemoaned or distressed, blamed others or flinched in the face of hindrances of any form.

Battle to Create New Heaven and Earth

Two years later, I took up appointment as dean of studies with a Taiwan Buddhist training program. But the position was terminated when the program was relocated from Hsinchu to Taipei and, essentially, because my views were deemed at the time too liberal. Some time afterwards, Venerable Yüan Jung's effort to recruit me for the faculty of Tung-shan Buddhist College was again thwarted by the objection of Master Tao Yüan, possibly for the same reason.

Instead of engaging myself in controversy, I thought, why would I not go and find a niche of my own elsewhere? That was when I decided to leave education and publishing to take up my position before the audience and spread the Dharma.

There in the ensuing thirty years were some of the lowest points in the course of my career as a speaker of the Dharma. My views were negated, my presence ostracized, my proposals for reform distorted, my appointments deterred, my travels obstructed, and my name smeared – time and again. Not that I was ever irked by such vicissitudes of life, I was merely saddened by the sorry state of the Buddhist circle at the time. Thus, for the freedom of development and the weal of all, I had to turn to the creation of another heaven and earth, and to strive on therein.

"In distance is manifested the potency of a steed; in gale is manifested the lifeforce of grass." Humanistic Buddhism, a concept much sneered at during those early years, has become a common goal shared by many. The last decade saw me busying myself in answer to requests to speak on the Dharma on all five continents and liaising with Buddhist bodies around the globe.

In perseverance I have proved that, despite affronting hindrances of all forms, there is neither need to plead for mercy nor to resist in anger. In the vow lies the primal force of motivation, which motorizes our mighty strokes up-stream; in agony lies renewed strength, which enables us to lift the looming clouds to once again let the sun shine through. In striving ahead, there is no need to be too humble or too proud. Select the good and attach to it. Help ourselves and help others. That way we shall not sweat in vain; others' affirmation will tell us so.

Slacken Not for a Moment

Perhaps political uncertainty and conceptual

difference are two of the most daunting stumbling blocks in the spread of the Dharma. I must mention that three decades ago the Christians were the only authorized evangelists in Taiwan and that even the few Buddhist telecasts, funded and produced independently, were banned – the reason being simply that Buddhist monks could not appear on television. Once I questioned the authorities thus: "Aren't those Buddhist monks, too, in the drama series?" The response was: "It is fine for the fake monks to preach, but not the real ones." On that note, I told myself: "The day will come when I shall turn the tide, eliminate the inequality, and eradicate the irony!"

Finally in 1979 the first Dharma telecast in the history of Chinese Buddhism was pioneered. A string of programs followed. These included *Kan-lu* (Sweet Dew), *Hsin-hsin mên* (Gate of Faith), *Hsing Yun Ch'an-hua* (Hsing Yun's Ch'an Talk), *Mei-jih yi-chieh* (A Verse Each Day), *Hsing Yun fa-yu* (Hsing Yun's Dharma Words), and other lectures on the sutras. They were broadcast on all three television stations, financed and facilitated by them. Transcripts of the programs sold tremendously well and copyrights to them were hotly sought after. As I witnessed how the society's attitude toward Buddhism changed from rejection to acceptance and from recognition to acclamation, I could not have been happier with the space we gained for the evolvement of our faith and with the reversal of the misunderstanding and negation of the early years. In charting new territories to spread the Dharma and, later, to organize other cultural and charitable undertakings, I must have also brought a certain share of pride to the Buddhist faith.

Wonderful as it is to found a temple and accommodate the sangha, it can also mean a lot of hassle. Fo Kuang Shan took nine years to obtain its official registration and Fu-shan Temple eight years. One of the most hairsplitting instants was when Yüan-fu Temple's premises were almost confiscated as a result of wranglings with the revenue department. In the days that followed, I chose to fight on the grounds of reason instead of resorting to lobbying through government channels as some disciples suggested I should. While pining for the outcome and braving one blow after another, I would also have to reassure my exasperated followers: "The officials have their terms to serve, but we monastics have a lifetime to give!" A temple, even flattened, can be reerected, but an aspiration, once declining, is as doomed as a rootless plant. Everything I do, I do for a lifetime; every battle I fight, I fight to the last breath. So far, has striving for aspiration not been well-proved to be so much richer in meaningfulness and worthiness than writhing in exasperation?

Historical records abound in instances of the Buddhas and Bodhisattvas unperturbed in the company of demons and of the ancestral masters undeviating in mayhem. Avowed out of compassion, they had committed body and mind to the continuation of Buddhism and the deliverance of all living beings. They, indeed, shall forever be my role models.

Ours are lamentable times! Many of us would not even blink in trading a lifetime's happiness for a moment's triumph or others' fortune for our own, or, ensnared in distress, we would throw up our arms too soon, displeasing friends, pleasing foes, and altogether doing no one any good. The plight at home wrings me; the impermanence of worldly affairs saddens me further. As the diverse pressures from international relations come encroaching on us, just how should the nation respond? Evasiveness and ignorance aside, surely neither foolhardiness nor fretfulness would make do. For only in striving to gain can we not lose, and in manifesting wisdom and solidarity can we be revered!

BEING USELESS,
BEING UNILLUMINED

Contrary to common scorn for uselessness, I see every reason to call uselessness the most useful.

A mighty useless fellow myself, I am a hopeless case in foreign languages. Course after course in English and Japanese still left me with little retention. Worst of all, having lived for forty-five years in Taiwan, this resident cannot even manage a decent phrase in the native dialect. Musically, I would as a rule stumble through the five tones[1] in Buddhist chanting, and I am virtually illiterate in reading scores. A professor of music once observed that I was capable of handling only three intonations,[2] and that the *ju* tone would forever be beyond reach. Altogether I do not even speak that well, being always too vocal in the defense of the right against wrong and hence having ruffled not a few feathers. The same openness has not waned as I advance in years, and it continues to become the cause of misconstruction and controversy. In monetary affairs, I am

[1] The pentatonic scale of do, re, mi, so, la.
[2] Out of the four intonations as in Mandarin.

practically thoughtless. Donations received in one hand would in no time be given away as a gift with the other. Many a time disciples and devotees would be worried sick over how constantly Fo Kuang Shan was in the red. But I have only the Dharma and somehow cannot seem to feel the angst of financial shortages as they do.

Practically useless I may be, I do embrace the wisdom of realizing my own limitations. Knowing that I am not brainy, I take no chances or shortcuts. Instead I take on the charges with both feet on the ground and always give my all. I treasure, most of all, every word of instruction bestowed upon me by teachers and superiors. At this point I must relate my encounter with Venerable Master T'ai Hsü, whom I had long admired. Then only eighteen, I remember gingerly walking up to him. Palms closed and absolutely overwhelmed, I prostrated in his presence. Smiling, he said repeatedly: "Good! Good! Good!" Then he walked on by. My mind was made up from that moment on: I will be *good* for the rest of my life. Thereafter I took to exercising discretion in whatever I said and did, reflecting on what I thought and how I behaved, practicing to perfect the Buddhist etiquette, and perusing all the Buddhist texts that came my way. I must say I owe all these to the handful of affirmations from Master T'ai Hsü.

Use Me and I'll be There

Not unnaturally for the robust twenty-three-year-old that I was when I settled in Chungli, the more taxing chores like pulling the cart and fetching water did fall on my shoulders. Somehow content to think myself pretty useless, I could not wait to be of use to others at all times and often exerted myself so much that I would be giddy and nauseous from exhaustion. I said little of either. That others found me usable, I knew in my heart of hearts, was adequately indicative of sterling worthfulness. Nobody should be let down in that regard! In the course of my preaching later on, too often I came to witness arrogance getting in the way of usefulness and talents fallen into disuse. How I, the less endowed, must be happy for what I am!

Much debate had I held with myself

over the appointment as dean of academic affairs and staff instructor in a Buddhist training program in Taiwan in 1951. I was verging on declining, knowing full well that I fell short both in Buddhist studies and wisdom. Then, I became aware of the severe shortage of those with the orthodox Buddhist education and training; I was appreciative, too, of the recognition given me. So I accepted. At the outset of the appointment, however, I ardently applied myself to the preparation of the pedagogy, building each example and researching every term just so no one was to be misguided.

The self-same meticulousness and quest for perfection continued through speech writing in the ensuing years. Verily the oratory that I have today stemmed from long periods of recompensing dullness with diligence. In the same token, six grinding years as editor and staff writer of two journals, *Chüeh-ch'ün* (Awakening the Masses) and *Jên-shêng* (Life Monthly), while teaching had provided me with ample opportunities to sharpen skills in writing and editing. Involvement in both fields despite personal shortfalls was due to the sad state that few others could and would likewise commit themselves. I remember sitting there and staring, for the longest time, at an unfinished line – called "vomiting my heart's energy and weeping blood." How wonderful that, as time goes by, I am able to pass on to disciples and followers the experience and knowledge accumulated in those areas!

It's Commitment That Counts

The first coordinating job for the rookie that I was in 1956 came from Chung-kuo Fo-chiao hui (Chinese Buddhist Association) for a major Dharma function. With little means other than the determination to reciprocate the trust so graciously bestowed on me, I went about rounding up as much help as possible and in the end brought the event to a success. A documentary was made and shown worldwide. It all added up to a pivotal achievement in my career. And, more than ever, I was led to believe that not being of much use matters little and that the sense of commitment is what really counts!

From the building of the temple in

Kaohsiung, the erecting of Shou-shan Temple, the founding of Fo Kuang Shan, to the establishment of a multitude of branch temples, I cannot recall how many construction projects I had partaken in. But I do remember treating each as though it were the first and only. Speculation would have no place in our operation; nor would inept reliance be placed on drafts and blueprints. I would myself expressly take time out of hectic schedules to inspect sites and work out the preliminaries in estimation and design. Such a hands-on approach was costly in time and manpower but realistic and thorough; the halls and chambers which went up as a result were blends of splendor and practicality, tradition and modernity.

Always at peace with my own lack of talent and virtue, I had since childhood aspired to burrowing through the biographies and records of ancient masters and sages for inspiration and endorsement, and patterning myself on the exemplars of judicious teachers and friends. In the conduction of the Buddhist affairs I would concentrate my energies on researching the pertinent management methods while recruiting extensive help and seeking expert consultation. A case in point is the establishment of the Buddhist college. In Buddhist studies, I am more of an eclectic than a specialist – that I know. I was trained exhaustively in the various schools, disciplines, and doctrines but am totally wanting in modern education – that I know, too. Hence a stream of seasoned scholars and brilliant young minds continue to be sought to fill the teaching posts in the Buddhist college, which subsequently continue to turn out the most promising graduates. It all tells me one thing: I may not be of much use to start, but in making good use of the useful, I can just as much partake in doing good to society and benefiting the sentient beings.

Admittedly, I have no qualms about seeking the advice of others and cross-references from other establishments. Manjusri,[3] extolled for his wisdom, was known to have prostrated at the feet of the maiden Miao-hui, then a mere eight-year-old, and sought her view on the Dharma. Ch'an

---

[3] Beautiful (Wonderful) Virtue (Fortune). The Bodhisattva symbolic of wisdom often seated on the left of Sakyamuni.

Master Chao Chou, at eighty, was still traveling about questing for teaching from the masters. For myself, I continue to cherish the camaraderie of scholars celebrated for their accomplishments and virtues, and together we have built for the past and shall continue to build for the futurity. "In the trio of which I am one, there must be a teacher for me." Respect for others not only makes up for personal weaknesses but also leads out the innermost strengths of all.

Each Little Cause, Every Little Condition

Each cause and every condition, however little, I hold dear to my heart; I cannot wait to share the joy, beauty, and facility of having. For knowing full well the least an average fellow like me can do is take everything and everyone seriously. With the same receptiveness I am prepared to treat a new acquaintance like an old friend, assuage a troubled soul who crosses my path, console the aged and inspire the young, and confer with political dignitaries and community leaders who care to come my way. As my followers multiply, my horizons broaden. Like a seemingly blasted woodland which, in its way, affords the openness and freedom for the formation of a pureland, from uselessness stems every possible use. Have no fear of being of not much use, therefore, for in so being, one is probably better positioned in humility to be receptive of causes and conditions of every kind.

Being useful in my uselessness has brought me much benefit. Better yet, every drip and drop of causes and conditions always add up to facilitate the spread of Buddhism and the weal of all living beings at large. Let me relate the recent fund-raising efforts we conducted for the Fo Kuang University foundation. The decision to employ the traditional alms-bowl,[4] to my utter astonishment, drew contribution, expertise, and volunteerism of all forms so much so that in six months an institution for higher learning is fast taking form. Personal limitations, no matter how crucial, can never curb the convergence of positive

---

[4] The Buddhist convention of monastics begging for sustenance from door to door.

forces and good affinities in the making of a magnificent cause.

Merits be to All

In the end I know that I am a taker much more than a giver. The sight of a Dharma function turning into a sensation or the sound of accolade humbles me so. In my heart of hearts I would pray that the merits be with others:

> Glory be to the Buddha, achievements be to all, benefits be to the monastery, merits be to the devotees.

Knowing one's own limitations is the key. Both in practice and in spreading the Dharma I have managed to do just that. I made it through the first ten years of monastic training with hearty acceptance of my own uselessness; the most arduous assignments and the harshest discipline, too, I accepted, thinking what must be would be. Those trials and errors turned out to be the unmeasured resources from which I would draw my strength in the struggles that awaited me.

What seemed like the rudest subjugation had blown into nothingness what I thought I knew and that ignorance born of the rise of conditions. How grateful I was to realize that!

I have made it through four decades of preaching the Dharma on the awareness of my own uselessness. I think often of the parents who gave me birth and reared me, the teachers who taught and guided me, the society which sustained me, and the Buddhist faith which furnished me with the space to grow in, and I am humbled to an excess for my inability to repay what I have taken. Thus, without ever blaming this bumpy life of mine on others, I continue to urge myself toward the next milestone down the road.

"You're right and I'm wrong; you're big and I'm small; you have and I haven't; joy be with you and pain be with me," I would often say, smiling at every injustice and acknowledging my own uselessness. For I have no way of competing with others; neither am I in any position to argue with anyone. Hence in paying a little more thought, waiting a little longer, giving up a little more of what I own, and parting with a little more wealth, I would be laying the groundwork for blessings and virtues, good causes and conditions. So far the outcome has proved me right: Injustice is a blessing.

Every so often ignorance gives rise to reproof. That I would tolerate as best I could, not out of feebleness and timidity, but because I know, in my uselessness, I must be at peace with myself and with others. So, instead of partaking in senseless wrangling, which could have further fueled a sensitive situation, I would add in a dash of humor or a few opportune words of Ch'an wisdom to reconnect with people around and reestablish harmony.

Refrain from Ignorance

Life's most insufferable malady is ignorance, not uselessness. Ignorance is the inability to understand how things come to be. It breeds defilements of all forms: greed, anger, foolishness, obsessiveness, doubts, and jealousy. Ignorance within displays itself without: a person walks about, poker-faced and taking offense with others in words and deeds. Called *wooden*, a *combative rooster,* or a *crow's beak* in the Taiwanese dialect, such a character, no matter how gifted, is short on good affinities and hence in accomplishments. I am afraid I do have a few like that among my followers. They think too highly of themselves and much too lowly of others; their ego, much overblown, gets in the way of teamwork; and their stubbornness obstructs their own progress. In fact, the usefulness of those who deem themselves useless becomes infinitely enhanced as a result of their open-mindedness, while that of those who deem themselves useful is often restricted as a result of their narrow-mindedness. That is my observation.

The few unillumined among my followers I take under my wings and, with personal guidance, they will all be brought to their senses. The evolvement never fails to amaze me. Asked how it is done, my answer is always simple. If only we can rekindle the blaze within us and let it consume the discrimination and ignorance therein, the inferior bits and pieces of ore can in the process turn into infrangible diamonds.

The least noticeable indeed is the little finger of the hand. But, palms closed in prayer, the little finger is closer to the Buddha than any other. No matter how insignificant we may seem, if only we act with the Buddha in our heart, accord with the Truth, count our blessings, be compassionate, and give generously, we are contributing to the good of all. The worst that can happen to anyone is to be shrouded in ignorance, unknowing of the existence of heavens and others beyond.

Remember the story about some men's foolhardy attempt to gauge the shape and size of an elephant by blind touch! Despite much time expended, conceit refrained them from reality and so in darkness they remained. Then again, there was the blind man fleeing the house on fire, who, fully aware of his own shortcomings, took to collaborating with his crippled and deaf buddies and so got the trio out of harm's way.

Ours are ever-changing times, escalated daily by horrendous information explosion such that the individual cannot be more negligible and ineffective. Hence we must not stop reflecting on and regretting for, really, how little we know, how much we are incapable of, and how impure and imperfect we are. Only in the sincerest repentance and ceaseless self-improvement can we gain in virtue and attain self-renewal; only in humility and self-restraint and with respect for those around us can affinity and collaboration bear the most wonderful fruit.

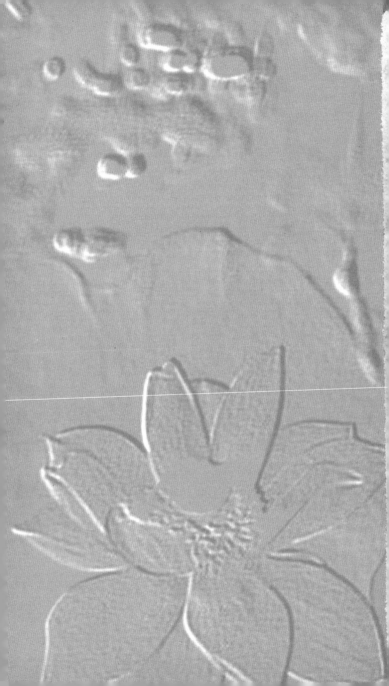